collections

Close Reader

Houghton
Mifflin
Harcourt

GRADE 10

Program Consultants:

Kylene Beers

Martha Hougen

Carol Jago

William L. McBride

Erik Palmer

Lydia Stack

Cover, Title Page Photo Credits: ©Pulse/Corbis

Printed in the U.S.A.

ISBN 978-0-544-08762-0

9 10 11 12   1421   19 18 17 16

4500595866   B C D E F G

COLLECTION 2
The Natural World

Visit hmhfyi.com for current articles and informational texts.

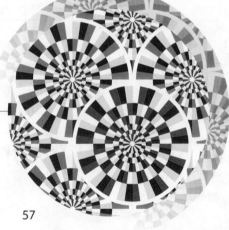

© Houghton Mifflin Harcourt Publishing Company • Image Credits: ©Dennis Novak/Photographer's Choice/Getty Images; ©Mark Grenier/Shutterstock

Visit hmhfyi.com
for current articles and
informational texts.

Becoming A Close Reader

READING THE TEXTS

Challenging literary and informational texts require close reading to understand and appreciate their meanings fully. These texts may have difficult language or complex structures that become clear only with careful study. To fully understand these demanding texts, you need to learn how to read and reread slowly and deliberately.

The Close Reader provides many opportunities to practice close reading. To become a close reader,

- read each text in the Close Reader slowly all the way through.
- take time to think about and respond to the READ and REREAD prompts that help focus your reading.
- cite specific textual evidence to support your analysis of the selection.

Your goal in close reading is to build useful knowledge as you analyze the author's message and appreciate the author's craft.

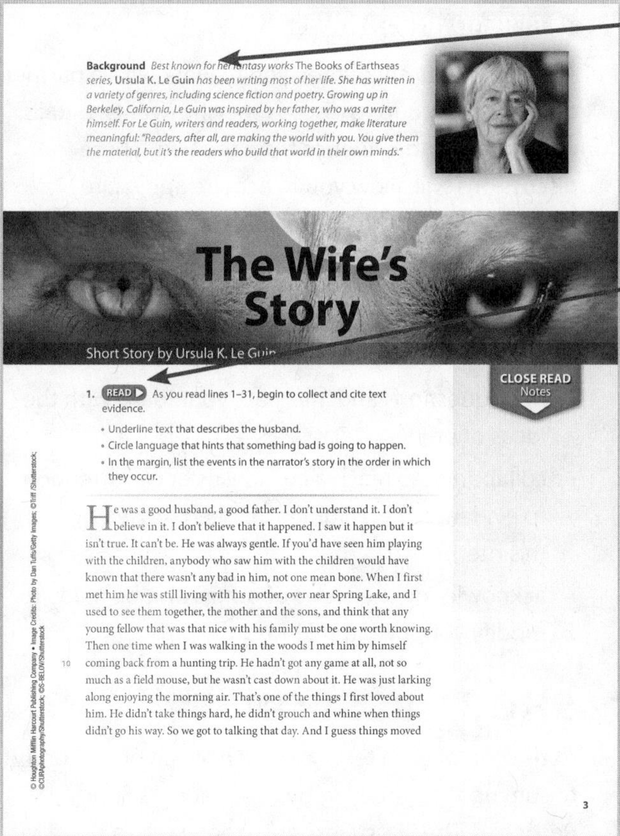

Background

This paragraph provides information about the text you are about to read. It helps you understand the context of the selection through additional information about the author, the subject, or the time period in which the text was written.

READER ►

With practice, you can learn how to be a close reader. Questions and specific instructions at the beginning of the selection and on the bottom of the pages will guide your close reading of each text.

These questions and instructions

- refer to specific sections of the text.
- ask you to look for and mark up specific information in the text.
- prompt you to record inferences and text analysis in the side margins.
- help you begin to collect and cite text evidence.

Vocabulary

Critical vocabulary words appear in the margin throughout most selections. Consult a print or online dictionary to define the word on your own.

When you see a vocabulary word in the margin,

- write the definition of each vocabulary word in the margin.
- be sure your definition fits the context of the word as it is used in the text.
- check your definition by substituting it in place of the vocabulary word from the text. Your definition should make sense in the context of the selection.

◄ REREAD

To further guide your close reading, REREAD questions at the bottom of the page will

- ask you to focus on a close analysis of a smaller chunk of text.
- prompt you to analyze literary elements and devices, as well as the meaning and structure of informational text.
- help you go back into the text and "read between the lines" to uncover possible meanings and central ideas.

Sample page content:

Background *Best known for her fantasy works The Books of Earthsea series,* **Ursula K. Le Guin** *has been writing most of her life. She has written in a variety of genres, including science fiction and poetry. Growing up in Berkeley, California, Le Guin was inspired by her father, who was a writer himself. For Le Guin, writers and readers, working together, make literature meaningful: "Readers, after all, are making the world with you. You give them the material, but it's the readers who build that world in their own minds."*

The Wife's Story

Short Story by Ursula K. Le Guin

CLOSE READ Notes

1. **READ ►** As you read lines 1–31, begin to collect and cite text evidence.
   - Underline text that describes the husband.
   - Circle language that hints that something bad is going to happen.
   - In the margin, list the events in the narrator's story in the order in which they occur.

He was a good husband, a good father. I don't understand it. I don't believe in it. I don't believe that it happened. I saw it happen but it isn't true. It can't be. He was always gentle. If you'd have seen him playing with the children, anybody who saw him with the children would have known that there wasn't any bad in him, not one mean bone. When I first met him he was still living with his mother, over near Spring Lake, and I used to see them together, the mother and the sons, and think that any young fellow that was that nice with his family must be one worth knowing. Then one time when I was walking in the woods I met him by himself coming back from a hunting trip. He hadn't got any game at all, not so much as a field mouse, but he wasn't cast down about it. He was just larking along enjoying the morning air. That's one of the things I first loved about him. He didn't take things hard, he didn't grouch and whine when things didn't go his way. So we got to talking that day. And I guess things moved

3

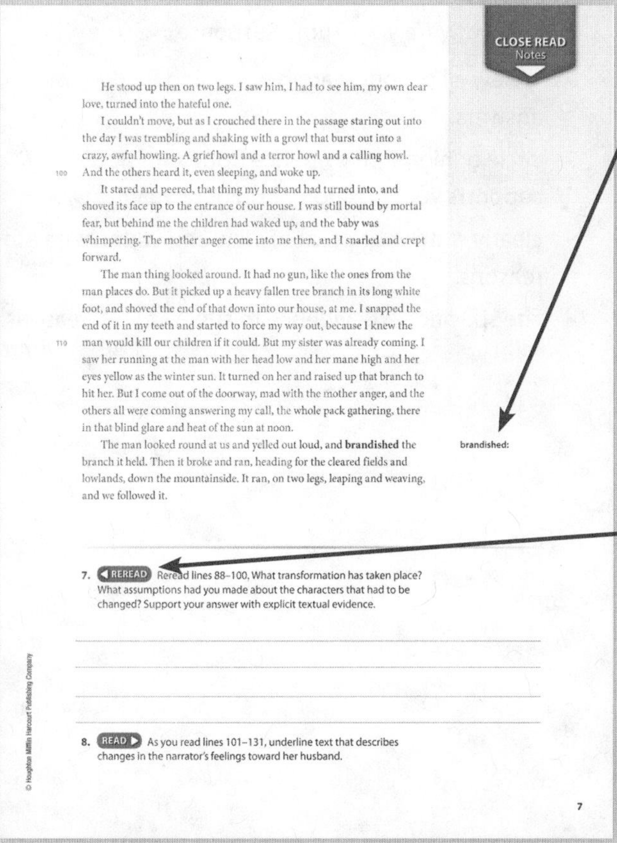

CLOSE READ Notes

He stood up then on two legs. I saw him, I had to see him, my own dear love, turned into the hateful one.

I couldn't move, but as I crouched there in the passage staring out into the day I was trembling and shaking with a growl that burst out into a crazy, awful howling. A grief howl and a terror howl and a calling howl. And the others heard it, even sleeping, and woke up.

It stared and peered, that thing my husband had turned into, and shoved its face up to the entrance of our house. I was still bound by mortal fear, but behind me the children had waked up, and the baby was whimpering. The mother anger come into me then, and I snarled and crept forward.

The man thing looked around. It had no gun, like the ones from the man places do. But it picked up a heavy fallen tree branch in its long white foot, and shoved the end of that down into our house, at me. I snapped the end of it in my teeth and started to force my way out, because I knew the man would kill our children if it could. But my sister was already coming. I saw her running at the man with her head low and her mane high and her eyes yellow as the winter sun. It turned on her and raised up that branch to hit her. But I come out of the doorway, mad with the mother anger, and the others all were coming answering my call, the whole pack gathering, there in that blind glare and heat of the sun at noon.

The man looked round at us and yelled out loud, and **brandished** the branch it held. Then it broke and ran, heading for the cleared fields and lowlands, down the mountainside. It ran, on two legs, leaping and weaving, and we followed it.

brandished:

7. **◄ REREAD** Reread lines 88–100. What transformation has taken place? What assumptions had you made about the characters that had to be changed? Support your answer with explicit textual evidence.

_____

_____

8. **READ ►** As you read lines 101–131, underline text that describes changes in the narrator's feelings toward her husband.

7

120   I was last, because love still bound the anger and the fear in me. I was running when I saw them pull it down. My sister's teeth were in its throat. I got there and it was dead. The others were drawing back from the kill, because of the taste of the blood, and the smell. The younger ones were cowering and some crying, and my sister rubbed her mouth against her forelegs over and over to get rid of the taste. I went up close because I thought if the thing was dead the spell, the curse must be done, and my husband could come back—alive, or even dead, if I could only see him, my true love, in his true form, beautiful. But only the dead man lay there white and bloody. We drew back and back from it, and turned and ran, back up

130   into the hills, back to the woods of the shadows and the twilight and the blessed dark.

9. ◀ **REREAD AND DISCUSS** Reread lines 120–131. With a small group, discuss why the wolves killed "the man thing." Do you think this was the right thing to do? Support your opinion with details from the story.

SHORT RESPONSE

Cite Text Evidence   Le Guin purposely misleads her reader as to the true identity of the narrator. How does this technique help the reader understand the motivation behind the narrator's action? **Cite text evidence** in your response.

_____

_____

_____

_____

_____

_____

_____

_____

_____

_____

8

◀ REREAD AND DISCUSS

These prompts encourage you to work with a partner or in a small group to discuss specific events, details, statements, and evidence from the text. These discussions will allow you to acquire and share knowledge about the texts you are reading.

As you engage in these discussions,

- be sure to cite specific text evidence in support of your statements.
- pose questions and integrate your ideas with the ideas of others.
- collaborate to reach a consensus or call attention to evidence that might have been missed or misinterpreted.
- acknowledge the views of others and be ready to modify your own thinking.

SHORT RESPONSE

At the end of each text, you will have an opportunity to sum up your thinking by completing a Short Response. The Short Response represents a place to convey some of the ideas you have developed through close reading of the text.

When you write your Short Response,

- review all of your margin notes and REREAD answers.
- circle or highlight evidence from your notes that supports your position or point of view.
- clearly state your point of view and support it with reasons.
- cite specific text evidence to support your reasons.

Ourselves and Others

Ourselves and Others

"We, as human beings, must be willing to accept people who are different from ourselves."

—Barbara Jordan

SHORT STORY
The Wife's Story

Ursula K. Le Guin

PUBLIC DOCUMENT
from the Universal Declaration of Human Rights

UN Commission on Human Rights

SPEECH
from Towards a True Refuge

Aung San Suu Kyi

Background *Best known for her fantasy works* The Books of Earthseas *series,* **Ursula K. Le Guin** *has been writing most of her life. She has written in a variety of genres, including science fiction and poetry. Growing up in Berkeley, California, Le Guin was inspired by her father, who was a writer himself. For Le Guin, writers and readers, working together, make literature meaningful: "Readers, after all, are making the world with you. You give them the material, but it's the readers who build that world in their own minds."*

The Wife's Story

Short Story by Ursula K. Le Guin

CLOSE READ
Notes

1. **READ** ▶ As you read lines 1–31, begin to collect and cite text evidence.

• Underline text that describes the husband.
• Circle language that hints that something bad is going to happen.
• In the margin, list the events in the narrator's story in the order in which they occur.

He was a good husband, a good father. I don't understand it. I don't believe in it. I don't believe that it happened. I saw it happen but it isn't true. It can't be. He was always gentle. If you'd have seen him playing with the children, anybody who saw him with the children would have known that there wasn't any bad in him, not one mean bone. When I first met him he was still living with his mother, over near Spring Lake, and I used to see them together, the mother and the sons, and think that any young fellow that was that nice with his family must be one worth knowing. Then one time when I was walking in the woods I met him by himself

10 coming back from a hunting trip. He hadn't got any game at all, not so much as a field mouse, but he wasn't cast down about it. He was just larking along enjoying the morning air. That's one of the things I first loved about him. He didn't take things hard, he didn't grouch and whine when things didn't go his way. So we got to talking that day. And I guess things moved

right along after that, because pretty soon he was over here pretty near all the time. And my sister said—see, my parents had moved out the year before and gone south, leaving us the place—my sister said, kind of teasing but serious, "Well! If he's going to be here every day and half the night, I guess there isn't room for me!" And she moved out—just down the way.

20 We've always been real close, her and me. That's the sort of thing doesn't ever change. I couldn't ever have got through this bad time without my sis.

Well, so he come to live here. And all I can say is, it was the happy year of my life. He was just purely good to me. A hard worker and never lazy, and so big and fine-looking. Everybody looked up to him, you know, young as he was. Lodge Meeting nights, more and more often they had him to lead the singing. He had such a beautiful voice, and he'd lead off strong, and the others following and joining in, high voices and low. It brings the shivers on me now to think of it, hearing it, nights when I'd stayed home from meeting when the children was babies—the singing coming up through the trees

30 there, and the moonlight, summer nights, the full moon shining. I'll never hear anything so beautiful. I'll never know a joy like that again.

It was the moon, that's what they say. It's the moon's fault, and the blood. It was in his father's blood. I never knew his father, and now I wonder what become of him. He was from up Whitewater way, and had no kin around here. I always thought he went back there, but now I don't know. There was some talk about him, tales, that come out after what happened to my husband. It's something runs in the blood, they say, and it may never come out, but if it does, it's the change of the moon that does it. Always it happens in the dark of the moon. When everybody's home and asleep.

40 Something comes over the one that's got the curse in his blood, they say,

2. **◀ REREAD** Reread lines 1–16, and think about how the narrator describes her husband. What do you learn about her character? Support your answer with explicit textual evidence.

_____

_____

_____

3. **READ ▶** As you read lines 32–58, continue to cite textual evidence.

• Underline text that hints that something bad is going to happen.
• Circle text that describes changes in the husband's behavior.
• In the margin, note what the narrator experiences directly.

> *Always it happens in the dark of the moon.*

and he gets up because he can't sleep, and goes out into the glaring sun, and goes off all alone—drawn to find those like him.

And it may be so, because my husband would do that. I'd half **rouse** and say, "Where you going to?" and he'd say, "Oh, hunting, be back this evening," and it wasn't like him, even his voice was different. But I'd be so sleepy, and not wanting to wake the kids, and he was so good and responsible, it was no call of mine to go asking "Why?'" and "Where?" and all like that.

So it happened that way maybe three times or four. He'd come back
50 late, and worn out, and pretty near cross for one so sweet-tempered—not wanting to talk about it. I figured everybody got to bust out now and then, and nagging never helped anything. But it did begin to worry me. Not so much that he went, but that he come back so tired and strange. Even, he smelled strange. It made my hair stand up on end. I could not endure it and I said, "What is that—those smells on you? All over you!" And he said, "I don't know," real short, and made like he was sleeping. But he went down when he thought I wasn't noticing, and washed and washed himself. But those smells stayed in his hair, and in our bed, for days.

And then the awful thing. I don't find it easy to tell about this. I want to
60 cry when I have to bring it to my mind. Our youngest, the little one, my baby, she turned from her father. Just overnight. He come in and she got scared-looking, stiff, with her eyes wide, and then she begun to cry and try to hide behind me. She didn't yet talk plain but she was saying over and over, "Make it go away! Make it go away!"

rouse:

---

4. ◀ **REREAD** Reread lines 43–58. How has the narrator's relationship with her husband changed? Support your answer with explicit textual evidence.

_____

_____

© Houghton Mifflin Harcourt Publishing Company • Image Credits: ©Triff/Shutterstock

The look in his eyes, just for one moment, when he heard that. That's what I don't want ever to remember. That's what I can't forget. The look in his eyes looking at his own child.

I said to the child, "Shame on you, what's got into you!"—scolding, but keeping her right up close to me at the same time, because I was frightened too. Frightened to shaking.

He looked away then and said something like, "Guess she just waked up dreaming." and passed it off that way. Or tried to. And so did I. And I got real mad with my baby when she kept on acting crazy scared of her own dad. But she couldn't help it and I couldn't change it.

He kept away that whole day. Because he knew, I guess. It was just beginning dark of the moon.

It was hot and close inside, and dark, and we'd all been asleep some while, when something woke me up. He wasn't there beside me. I heard a little stir in the passage, when I listened. So I got up, because I could bear it no longer. I went out into the passage, and it was light there, hard sunlight coming in from the door. And I saw him standing just outside, in the tall grass by the entrance. His head was hanging. Presently he sat down, like he felt weary, and looked down at his feet. I held still, inside, and watched—I didn't know what for.

And I saw what he saw. I saw the changing. In his feet, it was, first. They got long, each foot got longer, stretching out, the toes stretching out and the foot getting long, and fleshy, and white. And no hair on them.

The hair begun to come away all over his body. It was like his hair fried away in the sunlight and was gone. He was white all over, then, like a worm's skin. And he turned his face. It was changing while I looked. It got flatter and flatter, the mouth flat and wide, and the teeth grinning flat and dull, and the nose just a knob of flesh with nostril holes, and the ears gone, and the eyes gone blue—blue, with white rims around the blue—staring at me out of that flat, soft, white face.

5. **READ ▶** Read lines 59–70. In the margin, explain what happens between the father and the child. Why does the narrator scold her child?

6. **READ ▶** As you read lines 71–100, continue to cite textual evidence.

- Underline the unexpected events the narrator witnesses.
- In the margin, write what you think is happening to the narrator's husband.

He stood up then on two legs. I saw him, I had to see him, my own dear love, turned into the hateful one.

I couldn't move, but as I crouched there in the passage staring out into the day I was trembling and shaking with a growl that burst out into a crazy, awful howling. A grief howl and a terror howl and a calling howl.
100 And the others heard it, even sleeping, and woke up.

It stared and peered, that thing my husband had turned into, and shoved its face up to the entrance of our house. I was still bound by mortal fear, but behind me the children had waked up, and the baby was whimpering. The mother anger come into me then, and I snarled and crept forward.

The man thing looked around. It had no gun, like the ones from the man places do. But it picked up a heavy fallen tree branch in its long white foot, and shoved the end of that down into our house, at me. I snapped the end of it in my teeth and started to force my way out, because I knew the
110 man would kill our children if it could. But my sister was already coming. I saw her running at the man with her head low and her mane high and her eyes yellow as the winter sun. It turned on her and raised up that branch to hit her. But I come out of the doorway, mad with the mother anger, and the others all were coming answering my call, the whole pack gathering, there in that blind glare and heat of the sun at noon.

The man looked round at us and yelled out loud, and **brandished** the branch it held. Then it broke and ran, heading for the cleared fields and lowlands, down the mountainside. It ran, on two legs, leaping and weaving, and we followed it.

brandished:

---

7. **◄ REREAD** Reread lines 88–100. What transformation has taken place? What assumptions had you made about the characters that had to be changed? Support your answer with explicit textual evidence.

_____

_____

_____

_____

8. **READ ▶** As you read lines 101–131, underline text that describes changes in the narrator's feelings toward her husband.

120   I was last, because love still bound the anger and the fear in me. I was running when I saw them pull it down. My sister's teeth were in its throat. I got there and it was dead. The others were drawing back from the kill, because of the taste of the blood, and the smell. The younger ones were cowering and some crying, and my sister rubbed her mouth against her forelegs over and over to get rid of the taste. I went up close because I thought if the thing was dead the spell, the curse must be done, and my husband could come back—alive, or even dead, if I could only see him, my true love, in his true form, beautiful. But only the dead man lay there white and bloody. We drew back and back from it, and turned and ran, back up

130   into the hills, back to the woods of the shadows and the twilight and the blessed dark.

9. ◄ **REREAD AND DISCUSS**   Reread lines 120–131. With a small group, discuss why the wolves killed "the man thing." Do you think this was the right thing to do? Support your opinion with details from the story.

SHORT RESPONSE

Cite Text Evidence   Le Guin purposely misleads her reader as to the true identity of the narrator. How does this technique help the reader understand the motivation behind the narrator's actions? **Cite text evidence** in your response.

_____

_____

_____

_____

_____

_____

_____

_____

_____

Background *As people around the world discovered the atrocities committed against millions of innocent people in World War II, many wanted to create a universal statement of human rights. With the formation of the United Nations in 1945, this became a possibility. With guidance from the UN and First Lady Eleanor Roosevelt, Chairperson of the UN Commission on Human Rights, such a document was formulated, and adopted on December 10, 1948. Following is the Preamble to the Declaration, which consists of a series of statements beginning "Whereas . . . . " These statements provide a rationale for the Declaration; that is, they say why such a Declaration is necessary.*

from the
Universal Declaration of Human Rights

Public Document by the UN Commission on Human Rights

CLOSE READ
Notes

1. **READ ▷** As you read lines 1–13, begin to collect and cite text evidence.

   • Underline what conditions are necessary for "freedom, justice, and peace."
   • Circle the text that describes the biggest goal of the people of the world.

Whereas recognition of the inherent dignity and of the equal and **inalienable** rights of all members of the human family is the foundation of freedom, justice and peace in the world,

Whereas disregard and contempt for human rights have resulted in barbarous acts which have outraged the conscience of mankind, and the advent of a world in which human beings shall enjoy freedom of speech and belief and freedom from fear and want has been proclaimed as the highest aspiration of the common people,

10　Whereas it is essential, if man is not to be compelled to have recourse, as a last resort, to rebellion against tyranny and oppression, that human rights should be protected by the rule of law,

Whereas it is essential to promote the development of friendly relations between nations,

inalienable:

2. **◀ REREAD** Reread lines 9–11. In the margin, explain what will happen without protection of human rights.

People will lose control to higher coorperations or the Government, cause we cant do anything else,

9

Whereas the people of the United Nations have in the Charter reaffirmed their faith in fundamental human rights, in the dignity and worth of the human person and in the equal rights of men and women and have determined to promote social progress and better standards of life in larger freedom,

20 Whereas Member States have pledged themselves to achieve, in co-operation with the United Nations, the promotion of universal respect for and observance of human rights and fundamental freedoms,

Whereas a common understanding of these rights and freedoms is of the greatest importance for the full realization of this pledge,

Now, Therefore, THE GENERAL ASSEMBLY proclaims THIS UNIVERSAL DECLARATION OF HUMAN RIGHTS as a common standard of achievement for all people and all nations, to the end that every individual and every organ of society, keeping this Declaration constantly in mind, shall strive by teaching and education to promote respect for these rights and freedoms and by progressive measures, national and

30 international, to secure their universal and effective recognition and observance, both among the peoples of Member States themselves and among the peoples of territories under their **jurisdiction**.

jurisdiction:

3. **READ ▷** As you read lines 14–32, continue to cite textual evidence. Underline the values and goals of this document.

4. **◁ REREAD AND DISCUSS** Reread lines 24–32. With a small group, discuss the "call to action" in this paragraph. How might World War II have influenced the writers of this document?

SHORT RESPONSE

Cite Text Evidence A seminal document establishes or defines principles that shape the way others think or act. Why do you think the Preamble from the Universal Declaration of Human Rights is considered a seminal document? **Cite text evidence** from the document to support your claim.

Because it sets a basis for other countries and how their People should be treated in their inviorment

Background *Aung San Suu Kyi is the chairperson of the National League for Democracy in Myanmar (formerly known as Burma). She was placed under house arrest for opposing the military government shortly before she received a majority of votes in Myanmar's 1990 general election. In 1991, she won the Nobel Peace Prize for her commitment to nonviolence, but was unable to accept the prize until 2012, after spending 15 years under house arrest. In 2012, Aung San Suu Kyi topped the* Foreign Policy *list of the Top 100 Global Thinkers. The following excerpt is from a speech she wrote during her time as a political prisoner.*

from

Towards a True Refuge

Speech by Aung San Suu Kyi

CLOSE READ
Notes

1. **READ ▶** As you read lines 1–16, begin to collect and cite text evidence.

   - Underline Suu Kyi's idea of the "greatest threats to global security."
   - Circle words describing things that do <u>not</u> lead to global security, or "true refuge."

It is perfectly natural that all people should wish for a secure refuge. It is unfortunate that in spite of strong evidence to the contrary, so many still act as though security would be guaranteed if they fortified themselves with an abundance of material possessions. The greatest threats to global security today come not from the economic deficiencies of the poorest nations but from religious, racial (or tribal) and political **dissensions** raging in those regions where principles and practices which could reconcile the diverse instincts and aspirations of mankind have been ignored, repressed or distorted. Man-made disasters are made by dominant individuals and

10   cliques which refuse to move beyond the autistic[1] confines of **partisan** interest. An eminent development economist has observed that the best defense against famine is an accountable government. It makes little political or economic sense to give aid without trying to address the circumstances that render aid ineffectual. No amount of material goods

dissensions:

partisan:

---

[1] **autistic:** in this context, "self-centered."

and technological know how will compensate for human irresponsibility and viciousness.

Developed and developing nations alike suffer as a result of policies removed from a framework of values which uphold minimum standards of justice and tolerance. The rapidity with which the old Soviet Union
20 splintered into new states, many of them stamped with a fierce racial assertiveness, illustrates that decades of authoritarian rule may have achieved uniformity and obedience but could not achieve long-term harmony or stability. Nor did the material benefits enjoyed under the relatively successful post-totalitarian state of Yugoslavia succeed in dissipating the psychological impress of brooding historical experience that has now led to some of the worst religious and ethnic violence the Balkans have ever witnessed. Peace, stability and unity cannot be bought or coerced; they have to be nurtured by promoting a sensitivity to human needs and respect for the rights and opinions of others. Diversity and dissent need not
30 inhibit the emergence of strong, stable societies, but inflexibility, narrowness and unadulterated materialism can prevent healthy growth. And when attitudes have been allowed to harden to the point that otherness becomes a sufficient reason for nullifying a person's claim to be treated as a fellow human being, the trappings of modern civilization crumble with frightening speed.

In the most troubled areas of the world reserves of tolerance and compassion disappear, security becomes nonexistent and creature comforts are reduced to a minimum—but stockpiles of weapons abound. As a system of values this is totally mad. By the time it is accepted that the only way out
40 of an impasse of hate, bloodshed and social and economic chaos created by men is for those men to get together to find a peaceful solution through dialogue and compromise, it is usually no longer easy to restore sanity. Those who have been conditioned by systems which make a mockery of the law by legalizing injustices and which attack the very foundations of harmony by perpetuating social, political and economic imbalances cannot adjust quickly—if at all—to the concept of a fair settlement which places general well-being and justice above partisan advantage.

2. **◄ REREAD** Reread lines 1–16. In the margin, paraphrase Suu Kyi's position in these lines.

3. **READ ▶** As you read lines 17–47, continue to cite textual evidence.

• Underline the claims that Suu Kyi makes.
• Circle the evidence presented to support those claims.

During the Cold War the iniquities of ruthless governments and armed groups were condoned for ideological reasons. The results have been far
50 from happy. Although there is greater emphasis on justice and human rights today, there are still ardent advocates in favor of giving priority to political and economic **expediency**—increasingly the latter. It is the old argument: achieve economic success and all else will follow. But even long-affluent societies are plagued by formidable social ills which have provoked deep anxieties about the future. And newly rich nations appear to be spending a significant portion of their wealth on arms and armies. Clearly there is no inherent link between greater prosperity and greater security and peace—or even the expectation of greater peace. Both prosperity and peace are necessary for the happiness of mankind, the one to
60 alleviate suffering, the other to promote tranquility. Only policies that place equal importance on both will make a truly richer world, one in which men can enjoy *chantha*[2] of the body and of the mind. The drive for economic progress needs to be tempered with an awareness of the dangers of greed and selfishness which so easily lead to narrowness and inhumanity. If peoples and nations cultivate a generous spirit which welcomes the happiness of others as an enhancement of the happiness of the self, many seemingly insoluble problems would prove less **intractable**.

Those who have worked with refugees are in the best position to know that when people have been stripped of all their material supports, there
70 only remain to sustain them the values of their cultural and spiritual inheritance. A tradition of sharing instilled by age-old beliefs in the joy of giving and the sanctity of compassion will move a homeless destitute to press a portion of his meager ration on strangers with all the grace and delight of one who has ample riches to dispense. On the other hand, predatory traits honed by a long-established habit of yielding to "every urge

expediency:

intractable:

---

[2] *chantha*: prosperity and general happiness.

---

4. ◀ REREAD Reread lines 36–47. Think about Suu Kyi's choice of words here. How would you describe her tone in this paragraph?

_____

_____

_____

_____

5. READ ▶ As you read lines 48–92, underline sentences in which the author both presents solutions and provides evidence.

of nature which made self-serving the essence of human life" will lead men to plunder fellow sufferers of their last pathetic possessions.

And of course the great majority of the world's refugees are seeking sanctuary from situations rendered untenable by a **dearth** of humanity

80 and wisdom.

dearth:

The dream of a society ruled by loving kindness, reason and justice is a dream as old as civilized man. Does it have to be an impossible dream? Karl Popper,[3] explaining his abiding optimism in so troubled a world as ours, said that the darkness had always been there but the light was new. Because it is new it has to be tended with care and diligence. It is true that even the smallest light cannot be extinguished by all the darkness in the world because darkness is wholly negative. It is merely an absence of light. But a small light cannot dispel acres of encircling gloom. It needs to grow stronger, to shed its brightness further and further. And people need to

90 accustom their eyes to the light to see it as a benediction[4] rather than a pain, to learn to love it. We are so much in need of a brighter world which will offer adequate refuge to all its inhabitants.

---

[3] **Karl Popper** (1902–1994): a Viennese-born philosopher who became a British subject.
[4] **benediction:** blessing.

---

6. **READ** ▷ Read lines 81–92 and underline Suu Kyi's hopes for the future.

7. ◁ **REREAD AND DISCUSS** Reread lines 81–92. With a small group, discuss Suu Kyi's conclusion. What does the word *light* mean in her conclusion? How can light grow enough to overcome darkness?

SHORT RESPONSE

Cite Text Evidence What is Aung San Suu Kyi arguing for and against? How does her word choice and tone affect her overall meaning? Review your reading notes and **cite text evidence** in your response.

She is arguing against the rules set by our governments. And how we should change our situations for the better of people for the future not just yourself.

The Natural World

The Natural World

"Wildness reminds us what it means to be human, what we are connected to rather than what we are separate from."

—Terry Tempest Williams

Writing About the Sea

POEM
Starfish
Lorna Dee Cervantes

POEM
Sea Stars
Barbara Hurd

BLOG
Emma Marris: In Defense of Everglades Pythons
Andrew C. Revkin

SHORT STORY
The Seventh Man
Haruki Murakami,

***translated by* Jay Rubin**

Background *The following two selections are examples of writing about the sea—in particular, the creatures known as sea stars, or starfish. The word starfish is misleading. Starfish are not actually fish but echinoderms, animals with spiny skeletons. Although starfish come in a wide range of sizes, most species are between eight and twelve inches in diameter and have five arms. Their colors range from brown to various shades of yellow, orange, and pink. Starfish are flexible and move by using the tube feet on the undersides of their arms.*

Writing About the Sea

Lorna Dee Cervantes *Growing up in San Jose, California, Lorna Dee Cervantes discovered literature by reading the books in the houses that her mother cleaned for a living. Cervantes completed her first collection of poetry when she was fifteen. Writing gave Cervantes, who is of Mexican and American Indian ancestry, a sense of freedom: "When you grow up as I did, a Chican-India in a barrio in a Mexican neighborhood in California . . . you're ignored . . . And you're not expected to speak, much less write."*

Barbara Hurd *is a writer who specializes in creative nonfiction nature writing. She explains, "I'm interested in landscapes, both the physical—swamps and caves—and the psychological, that are marked by multiplicities and contradictions, pocked with secrets, laced with what can't be immediately seen, but, which properly pressed by imagination and language, have the power to transform experience into something sculpted and meaningful. . . . I'm after form, in other words, which leaves the reader and me at least knee-deep in this world, aware of and almost weaker than the wish to resist."*

1. **READ ▶** As you read lines 1–15 of "Starfish," begin to cite text evidence.

   - Underline examples of figurative language.
   - Circle text used to describe the starfish's body.
   - In the margin, explain the actions of the speaker.

Starfish
Lorna Dee Cervantes

They were lovely in the quartz and jasper sand
As if they had created terrariums[1] with their bodies
On purpose; adding sprigs of seaweed, seashells,
White feathers, eel bones, miniature
5   Mussels, a fish jaw. Hundreds; no—
Thousands of baby stars. We touched them,
Surprised to find them soft, **pliant**, almost
Living in their attitudes. We would dry them, arrange them,
Form seascapes, geodesics[2] . . . We gathered what we could
10   In the approaching darkness. Then we left hundreds of
Thousands of flawless five-fingered specimens sprawled
Along the beach as far as we could see, all massed
Together: little martyrs, soldiers, artless suicides
In lifelong liberation from the sea. So many
15   Splayed hands, the tide shoveled in.

pliant:

_____

[1] **terrarium:** small enclosure or container that houses plants or animals.
[2] **geodesic:** interlocking, repeating pattern.

2. **◀ REREAD** Reread lines 1–15. How does the description of the "approaching darkness" change the tone of the poem? What happens to the starfish the speaker leaves behind? Support your answer with explicit text evidence.

_____

_____

_____

_____

SHORT RESPONSE

Cite Text Evidence   How does the poet's use of figurative language contribute
to her central idea? **Cite text evidence** to support your response.

_____

_____

_____

_____

_____

_____

_____

_____

_____

_____

1. **READ ▷** As you read lines 1–12 of "Sea Stars," begin to cite text evidence.

   - Underline words and phrases used to describe the sky, the moon, and the stars.
   - Circle text that gives the sea stars human qualities.
   - In the margin, explain the comparison the author makes.

Sea Stars
Barbara Hurd

The sky is pink this morning and on the shore a whole host[1] of sea stars has been stranded.

I know from the charts the moon was full last night, the midnight tide higher than usual. Were the skies clear? Were the stars out? I'd like to have seen these creatures then: stars in the dark overhead and here a spiny constellation draped over the rocks.

One of the largest, a northern sea star, now lies upside down in the palm of my hand. Almost a foot across, its orangy body glistens wet in the dawn light. Hundreds of slender tubes wriggle like antennae, only these
10 aren't sense organs; they're feet, and what they're searching for isn't food or enemy or mate, but something to cling to, any firm surface that can anchor them and end this **futile** flailing at the air.

Of its five arms, three remain, five or six inches long. I've read that most sea stars lose their limbs to other sea stars' hunger. Traveling in slow-motion swarms, the lead **contingent** feasts on oysters and clams, depleting the supply for those in the rear, who resort to the nearest neighbor's arm.

futile:

contingent:

---

[1] **host:** an army, group or formation.

2. **◁ REREAD** Reread lines 1–12. In your own words, explain the central idea of these lines.

_____

_____

_____

_____

3. **READ ▷** As you read lines 13–26, continue to cite text evidence.

   - Underline facts about the life cycle of the sea star.
   - Circle emotions that humans are "burdened" with.
   - In the margin, explain the physical feeling that both amputees and people born without a limb may have in common.

The sea star, of course, can regenerate[2] when the food supply increases, grow back the missing limb, and continue unburdened by notions of heroism or sacrifice, even consciousness.

20   We, in contrast, have to live with those burdens, made heavier by loss and the sensation that often emanates from what's missing. Amputees[3] call it phantom pain, those sensations—tingling or sharp stabs—by which something absent makes its presence known. Even those born without a limb sometimes feel what was never there and experience, physically, what others of us know psychologically—a need to confirm what we feel but can't see.

When its third arm begins to wriggle, I turn the sea star over and carry it back to the water. Oblivious to patience or my unreliable intentions, it knows only the dangers of drying out set against the dangers of being
30   washed out to sea. I try to imagine that twice-daily rhythm, sun on its baking back, tube feet squishing as it inches along among drying seaweed and barnacles. And then the fierce holding on as the tide comes in and wave after wave crashes on top of delicate tissues.

Were the stars out last night? Silly question, really. They're always out. In the daytime too. Where do we think they'd go? I try to remember this: the obscuring effect of clouds and of sunlight, how things that seem to disappear often have not. Up in the daytime sky, the whirling constellations—Cassiopeia, Orion, Big Dipper—may be invisible to us, but stage a noontime solar eclipse and there they are, as always, reminders of
40   other worlds we'll probably never see. And here, underfoot, half a dozen sea

---

[2] **regenerate:** to replace a lost or damaged part by forming new tissue.
[3] **amputee:** a person who has had one or more limbs removed.

---

4. **◀ REREAD** Reread lines 13–26. What point is the author making by comparing a sea star missing an arm to a human missing a limb?

_____

_____

_____

_____

5. **READ ▶** As you read lines 27–58, continue to cite text evidence.

• Underline the "twice-daily rhythm" the author describes in lines 30–33.

• Circle the idea the author tries to remember.

• In the margin, explain the author's answers to the questions she poses in lines 34–35.

stars, about to disappear underwater where they'll go on too, misshapen maybe and less visible, doing what they've always done: making their slow way through a galaxy spread out at our feet.

Foaming and inching its lunar way up the beach, the sea polishes small stones, sloshes into and out of the tiny whorled and bivalved[4] shells somersaulting in the undercurl of its waves. I take it as a given we can't escape the way the world grinds the living into debris. But before it does, there's a chance for the lucky encounter with someone or something—a painting or poem, a place—that can beckon to what lies broken and hungry inside us all. I believe it's what most of us long for.

Oh Ahab,[5] I often think, if you could have hunted with less vengeance and fewer absolutes, might the whale have someday returned to you what it took so long ago, so violently? Not literally, no leg, of course. Not even in a story would anyone believe a human could do what a sea star can. But something else, something **elusive** that retreats in the onslaught of high drama and fierce truths, that survives between the layers of the said and the felt, and makes itself known to us only by the ghostly presence of its wanting.

---

[4] **bivalve:** a class of mollusks characterized by a hinged shell.

[5] **Ahab:** the main character from Herman Melville's *Moby Dick*, whose main purpose in life is to seek out and destroy the giant whale that bit off his leg.

elusive:

50

CLOSE READ
Notes

6. **◄ REREAD** Reread lines 27–58. In the margin, explain what the author wants to say to Ahab in lines 51–58.

SHORT RESPONSE

Cite Text Evidence In what ways does the author's use of figurative language contribute to her central idea? **Cite text evidence** to support your response.

22

© Houghton Mifflin Harcourt Publishing Company

Background *The Everglades are a natural region of wetlands located in southern Florida. For nearly 100 years, scientists and environmental activists have been focused on saving this "River of Grass" from investors eager to drain it for land development. Today, however, there is a new threat to the Everglades—the human introduction of nonnative predators, such as the Burmese python, to this fragile ecosystem. In this follow-up to a post he had written for the* Dot Earth *blog of* The New York Times, *environmental reporter* **Andrew C. Revkin** *presents enviromental author Emma Marris's response to the issue.*

Emma Marris:
In Defense of Everglade Pythons

Blog by Andrew C. Revkin

1. **READD ▶** As you read lines 1–11, begin to collect and cite text evidence.

   - Underline information in the first paragraph that summarizes Revkin's first post about the python.
   - Circle persuasive language that Revkin uses to convince readers that the response to his post is interesting.
   - In the margin, explain how the use of the word *plight* in line 10 expresses Revkin's point of view.

CLOSE READ
Notes

Here's a fascinating "Your Dot" followup to my post on the 17-foot egg-bearing female Burmese python that was caught, tracked and euthanized by federal biologists working to understand the impact of this introduced predator on the Everglades and Florida. I sent the piece to a variety of biologists and scholars focused on the strange ecology of this Anthropocene[1] era in which so many Earth systems are increasingly under our sway.

Emma Marris, the author of one of my favorite books of the last few years, "Rambunctious Garden: Saving Nature in a Post-Wild World," sent
10 this provocative reflection on the plight of the python, which—because of humans' penchant for exotic pets—has become such a "movable beast":

---

[1] **Anthropocene:** an informal name for a new geologic era referred to as the Age of Man. This new era is defined by the impact of human activities on Earth's ecosystems.

* * *

defile:

I think that the pythons in the Everglades fascinate us not only because enormous pythons are intrinsically mesmerizing, but because they echo the old biblical story of the serpent in Eden, a nasty outsider **defiling** paradise and ruining everything. Of course, the notion of the Everglades as a paradise is relatively new. We used to think of the place as a "worthless

morass:

morass," as Michael Grunwald put it in his book on the history of the Everglades. The idea that marshes and swamps are places of natural beauty is less than 100 years old.

20   But now that the Everglades has become an international treasure, these snakes, which are just doing what they evolved to do as they pig out on the native fauna, have been painted as evil and despicable. It's the blame-the-invasive species narrative that's been in fashion for a few decades now, here helped out by the fact that many people have a visceral ick or eek reaction to snakes. But it isn't the pythons' fault. It is our fault for introducing them.

Yes, insofar as they threaten native species in the Everglades, I wish we could undo that mistake and remove them all. But it ain't gonna happen. And so, I suggest, we might try to learn to love the pythons rather than

revile:

revile them. They are really impressive beasts. This doesn't mean we

30   shouldn't necessarily try to control their numbers as part of an overall management strategy, but it might mean that if you are touring the

2. **◀ REREAD** Reread lines 1–7. What is the author's attitude toward human activity and its impact on the environment? Support your answer with explicit textual evidence.

_____

_____

_____

_____

3. **READ ▶** As you read lines 12–25, continue to cite text evidence.

• Underline the reason Marris gives for our fascination with pythons in the Everglades.

• Underline the claim Marris makes in lines 20–25 and paraphrase it in the margin.

• Circle the phrase in lines 20–25 that Marris uses to describe the situation.

"But it isn't the pythons' fault. It is our fault for introducing them."

Everglades and you see one, you might consider yourself lucky, rather than grimacing and feeling that the purity of your experience was somehow tainted.

The pythons came up at this June's Aspen Environment Forum. I got into a debate with E. O. Wilson about the Everglades [*during this session*]. He believes (more or less) that we should be going in there guns blazing, get every last python out, and keep the River of Grass "pure." I suggested that the pythons were likely here to stay no matter how hard we tried and that
40 the effort would likely be wasted, since the Everglades will probably be underwater in a few generations anyway, thanks to climate-change induced sea level rise. I said we should focus on protecting areas uphill so the species we like in the marsh have somewhere to go. He then suggested I was carrying around a white flag of surrender, and I rejoined that I never enlisted in the war for "purity" as defined by the world as it was in 1492, that rather I fought for Nature as a dynamic and mutable thing. And then the buzzer sounded and we both went back to our corners to get toweled off.

4. ◀ **REREAD** Reread lines 12–19. What evidence does Marris use to support her claim that the "notion of the Everglades as a paradise is relatively new"?

_____

_____

_____

_____

_____

5. **READ** ▶ Read lines 26–57 and continue to cite evidence.

• Underline Marris's counterarguments to E. O. Wilson.

• In the margin, restate Wilson's viewpoints.

It is possible that I am being too accepting of change here. This is the Everglades we are talking about, and there are so many people who have

50 fallen in love with the particular constellation of species that were there when Europeans first came to this continent, that it might be worth fighting very hard to keep it that way. Maybe I am going overboard on my "learn to love the inevitable changes" mantra. But it is really how I feel. If the choice is to fight for a pure Everglades and lose, or to work with nature as it changes and adapts to what we humans have done to planet Earth, respecting its dynamism and resilience as it shifts to new states, I vote for the latter. Just don't call me a python hugger. That sounds painful.

6. ◀ **REREAD** Reread lines 35–57. In your own words, restate Marris's opinions about change.

_____

_____

_____

SHORT RESPONSE

Cite Text Evidence Did Marris convince you that the pythons should be allowed to stay in the Everglades? Explain, **citing text evidence** in your response.

_____

_____

_____

_____

_____

_____

_____

_____

Background *As a boy,* **Haruki Murakami** *preferred reading American paperbacks to studying traditional Japanese literature. He went on to become a novelist and short-story writer known for unique and whimsical works that break away from typical Japanese forms. Murakami combines mystery, comedy, and fantasy in his work, while keeping his messages practical, profound, and believable.*

The Seventh Man

Short Story by Haruki Murakami   translated by Jay Rubin

CLOSE READ
Notes

1. **READ ▷** As you read lines 1–30, begin to collect and cite text evidence.

   • Circle text in lines 1–15 that creates a mood. In the margin, describe that mood.
   • Underline examples of figurative language: personification, simile, and metaphor.
   • In lines 16–30, circle text that makes the seventh man seem mysterious.

"A huge wave nearly swept me away," said the seventh man, almost whispering.

"It happened one September afternoon when I was ten years old."

The man was the last one to tell his story that night. The hands of the clock had moved past ten. The small group that huddled in a circle could hear the wind tearing through the darkness outside, heading west. It shook the trees, set the windows to rattling, and moved past the house with one final whistle.

"It was the biggest wave I had ever seen in my life," he said. "A strange wave. An absolute giant."

He paused.

"It just barely missed me, but in my place it swallowed everything that mattered most to me and swept it off to another world. I took years to find it again to recover from the experience—precious years that can never be replaced."

10

The seventh man appeared to be in his mid-fifties. He was a thin man, tall, with a moustache, and next to his right eye he had a short but deep-looking scar that could have been made by the stab of a small blade. Stiff, bristly patches of white marked his short hair. His face had the look you see
20 on people when they can't quite find the words they need. In his case, though, the expression seemed to have been there from long before, as though it were part of him. The man wore a simple blue shirt under a grey tweed coat, and every now and then he would bring his hand to his collar. None of those assembled there knew his name or what he did for a living.

He cleared his throat, and for a moment or two his words were lost in silence. The others waited for him to go on.

"In my case, it was a wave," he said. "There's no way for me to tell, of course, what it will be for each of you. But in my case it just happened to take the form of a gigantic wave. It presented itself to me all of a sudden one
30 day, without warning. And it was devastating."

I grew up in a seaside town in the Province of S. It was such a small town, I doubt that any of you would recognize the name if I were to mention it. My father was the local doctor, and so I led a rather comfortable childhood. Ever since I could remember, my best friend was a boy I'll call K. His house was close to ours, and he was a grade behind me in school. We were like brothers, walking to and from school together, and always playing together when we got home. We never once fought during our long

---

2. **◀ REREAD** Reread lines 16–30. Explain what the wave might symbolize to Murakami.

_____

_____

_____

_____

_____

3. **READ ▶** As you read lines 31–58, continue to cite text evidence.

• In the margin, explain how the structure of the story changes in line 31.
• Underline text that describes the narrator's relationship with K.

© Houghton Mifflin Harcourt Publishing Company

friendship. I did have a brother, six years older, but what with the age difference and differences in our personalities, we were never very close. My
40   real brotherly affection went to my friend K.

     K. was a frail, skinny little thing, with a pale complexion and a face almost pretty enough to be a girl's. He had some kind of speech **impediment**, though, which might have made him seem retarded to anyone who didn't know him. And because he was so frail, I always played his protector, whether at school or at home. I was kind of big and athletic, and the other kids all looked up to me. But the main reason I enjoyed spending time with K. was that he was such a sweet, pure-hearted boy. He was not the least bit retarded, but because of his impediment, he didn't do too well at school. In most subjects, he could barely keep up. In art class, though, he
50   was great. Just give him a pencil or paints and he would make pictures that were so full of life that even the teacher was amazed. He won prizes in one contest after another, and I'm sure he would have become a famous painter if he had continued with his art into adulthood. He liked to do seascapes. He'd go out to the shore for hours, painting. I would often sit beside him, watching the swift, precise movements of his brush, wondering how, in a few seconds, he could possibly create such lively shapes and colors where, until then, there had been only blank white paper. I realize now that it was a matter of pure talent.

     One year, in September, a huge typhoon hit our area. The radio said it
60   was going to be the worst in ten years. The schools were closed, and all the shops in town lowered their shutters in preparation for the storm. Starting early in the morning, my father and brother went around the house nailing shut all the storm doors, while my mother spent the day in the kitchen cooking emergency provisions. We filled bottles and canteens with water, and packed our most important possessions in rucksacks for possible evacuation. To the adults, typhoons were an annoyance and a threat they had to face almost annually, but to the kids, removed as we were from such practical concerns, it was just a great big circus, a wonderful source of excitement.

70   Just after noon the color of the sky began to change all of a sudden. There was something strange and unreal about it. I stayed outside on the porch, watching the sky, until the wind began to howl and the rain began to

impediment:

---

4. **READ ▶** As you read lines 59–118, continue to cite text evidence.

   • Underline figurative language, including similes, metaphors, personification, and idioms.

   • In the margin, explain the images this language evokes.

beat against the house with a weird dry sound, like handfuls of sand. Then we closed the last storm door and gathered together in one room of the darkened house, listening to the radio. This particular storm did not have a great deal of rain, it said, but the winds were doing a lot of damage, blowing roofs off houses and capsizing ships. Many people had been killed or injured by flying debris. Over and over again, they warned people against leaving their homes. Every once in a while, the house would creak and

80 shudder as if a huge hand were shaking it, and sometimes there would be a great crash of some heavy-sounding object against a storm door. My father guessed that these were tiles blowing off the neighbors' houses. For lunch we ate the rice and omelettes my mother had cooked, waiting for the typhoon to blow past.

But the typhoon gave no sign of blowing past. The radio said it had lost momentum almost as soon as it came ashore at S. Province, and now it was moving north-east at the pace of a slow runner. The wind kept up its savage howling as it tried to uproot everything that stood on land.

Perhaps an hour had gone by with the wind at its worst like this when

90 a hush fell over everything. All of a sudden it was so quiet, we could hear a bird crying in the distance. My father opened the storm door a crack and looked outside. The wind had stopped, and the rain had ceased to fall. Thick, grey clouds edged across the sky, and patches of blue showed here and there. The trees in the yard were still dripping their heavy burden of rainwater.

"We're in the eye of the storm," my father told me. "It'll stay quiet like this for a while, maybe fifteen, twenty minutes, kind of like an intermission. Then the wind'll come back the way it was before."

I asked him if I could go outside. He said I could walk around a little if I

100 didn't go far. "But I want you to come right back here at the first sign of wind."

I went out and started to explore. It was hard to believe that a wild storm had been blowing there until a few minutes before. I looked up at the sky. The storm's great "eye" seemed to be up there, fixing its cold stare on all of us below. No such "eye" existed, of course: we were just in that momentary quiet spot at the center of the pool of whirling air.

While the grown-ups checked for damage to the house, I went down to the beach. The road was littered with broken tree branches, some of them thick pine boughs that would have been too heavy for an adult to lift alone.

110 There were shattered roof tiles everywhere, cars with cracked windshields,

and even a doghouse that had tumbled into the middle of the street. A big hand might have swung down from the sky and flattened everything in its path.

K. saw me walking down the road and came outside.

"Where are you going?" he asked.

"Just down to look at the beach," I said.

Without a word, he came along with me. He had a little white dog that followed after us.

"The minute we get any wind, though, we're going straight back home," I said, and K. gave me a silent nod.

120

The shore was a 200-yard walk from my house. It was lined with a concrete breakwater—a big **dyke** that stood as high as I was tall in those days. We had to climb a short flight of steps to reach the water's edge. This was where we came to play almost every day, so there was no part of it we didn't know well. In the eye of the typhoon, though, it all looked different: the color of the sky and of the sea, the sound of the waves, the smell of the tide, the whole expanse of the shore. We sat atop the breakwater for a time, taking in the view without a word to each other. We were supposedly in the middle of a great typhoon, and yet the waves were strangely hushed. And

130

the point where they washed against the beach was much farther away than usual, even at low tide. The white sand stretched out before us as far as we could see. The whole, huge space felt like a room without furniture, except for the band of **flotsam** that lined the beach.

dyke:

flotsam:

5. **◀ REREAD** Reread lines 96–118. How does the author foreshadow the danger to come? Support your answer with explicit textual evidence.

_____

_____

_____

_____

6. **READ ▶** As you read lines 119–159, continue to cite text evidence.

- Circle references to soundlessness.
- Continue to underline figurative language: idioms, similes, metaphors, personification.
- In the margin, explain the impact of the figurative language the author uses.

> ❝ *The sea had suddenly stretched its long, smooth tonuge out to where I stood on the beach.* ❞

We stepped down to the other side of the breakwater and walked along the broad beach, examining the things that had come to rest there. Plastic toys, sandals, chunks of wood that had probably once been parts of furniture, pieces of clothing, unusual bottles, broken crates with foreign writing on them, and other, less recognizable items: it was like a big candy store. The storm must have carried these things from very far away.

140   Whenever something unusual caught our attention, we would pick it up and look at it every which way, and when we were done, K.'s dog would come over and give it a good sniff.

We couldn't have been doing this more than five minutes when I realized that the waves had come up right next to me. Without any sound or other warning, the sea had suddenly stretched its long, smooth tongue out to where I stood on the beach. I had never seen anything like it before. Child though I was, I had grown up on the shore and knew how frightening the ocean could be—the savagery with which it could strike unannounced.

And so I had taken care to keep well back from the waterline. In spite of

150   that, the waves had slid up to within inches of where I stood. And then, just as soundlessly, the water drew back—and stayed back. The waves that had approached me were as unthreatening as waves can be—a gentle washing of the sandy beach. But something ominous about them—something like the touch of a reptile's skin—had sent a chill down my spine. My fear was totally groundless—and totally real. I knew instinctively that they were alive. They knew I was here and they were planning to grab me. I felt as if some huge, man-eating beast were lying somewhere on a grassy plain, dreaming of the moment it would pounce and tear me to pieces with its sharp teeth. I had to run away.

160   "I'm getting out of here!" I yelled to K. He was maybe ten yards down the beach, squatting with his back to me, and looking at something. I was sure I had yelled loud enough, but my voice did not seem to have reached him. He might have been so absorbed in whatever it was he had found that my call made no impression on him. K. was like that. He would get involved with things to the point of forgetting everything else. Or possibly I had not yelled as loudly as I had thought. I do recall that my voice sounded strange to me, as though it belonged to someone else.

    Then I heard a deep rumbling sound. It seemed to shake the earth. Actually, before I heard the rumble I heard another sound, a weird gurgling
170 as though a lot of water was surging up through a hole in the ground. It continued for a while, then stopped, after which I heard the strange rumbling. Even that was not enough to make K. look up. He was still squatting, looking down at something at his feet, in deep concentration. He probably did not hear the rumbling. How he could have missed such an earth-shaking sound, I don't know. This may seem odd, but it might have been a sound that only I could hear—some special kind of sound. Not even K.'s dog seemed to notice it, and you know how sensitive dogs are to sound.

    I told myself to run over to K., grab hold of him, and get out of there. It was the only thing to do. I *knew* that the wave was coming, and K. didn't
180 know. As clearly as I knew what I ought to be doing, I found myself running the other way—running full speed toward the dyke, alone. What made me do this, I'm sure, was fear, a fear so overpowering it took my voice away and set my legs to running on their own. I ran stumbling along the soft sand beach to the breakwater, where I turned and shouted to K.

---

7. ◀ **REREAD AND DISCUSS**   Reread lines 149–159. With a small group, discuss what the narrator means when he says he "knew" that the waves were alive.

8. **READ** ▷   As you read lines 160–205, continue to cite text evidence.

- Circle meaningful references to sound or soundlessness.
- In the margin, explain what happens to K.

"Hurry, K.! Get out of there! The wave is coming!" This time my voice worked fine. The rumbling had stopped, I realized, and now, finally, K. heard my shouting and looked up. But it was too late. A wave like a huge snake with its head held high, poised to strike, was racing towards the shore. I had never seen anything like it in my life. It had to be as tall as a three-story building. Soundlessly (in my memory, at least, the image is soundless), it rose up behind K. to block out the sky. K. looked at me for a few seconds, uncomprehending. Then, as if sensing something, he turned towards the wave. He tried to run, but now there was no time to run. In the next instant, the wave had swallowed him.

The wave crashed on to the beach, shattering into a million leaping waves that flew through the air and plunged over the dyke where I stood. I was able to dodge its impact by ducking behind the breakwater. The spray wet my clothes, nothing more. I scrambled back up on to the wall and scanned the shore. By then the wave had turned and, with a wild cry, it was rushing back out to sea. It looked like part of a gigantic rug that had been yanked by someone at the other end of the earth. Nowhere on the shore could I find any trace of K., or of his dog. There was only the empty beach.

9. **◄ REREAD** Reread lines 160–205. Why do you think the narrator fails to rescue K? What else does the narrator have problems doing?

_____

_____

_____

© Houghton Mifflin Harcourt Publishing Company • Image Credits: ©natureslight/Alamy

The receding wave had now pulled so much water out from the shore that it seemed to expose the entire ocean bottom. I stood along on the breakwater, frozen in place.

The silence came over everything again—a desperate silence, as though sound itself had been ripped from the earth. The wave had swallowed K. and disappeared into the far distance. I stood there, wondering what to do. Should I go down to the beach? K. might be down there somewhere, buried in the sand . . . But I decided not to leave the dyke. I knew from experience that big waves often came in twos and threes.

I'm not sure how much time went by—maybe ten or twenty seconds of eerie emptiness—when, just as I had guessed, the next wave came. Another gigantic roar shook the beach, and again, after the sound had faded, another huge wave raised its head to strike. It towered before me, blocking out the sky, like a deadly cliff. This time, though, I didn't run. I stood rooted to the sea wall, entranced, waiting for it to attack. What good would it do to run, I thought, now that K. had been taken? Or perhaps I simply froze, overcome with fear. I can't be sure what it was that kept me standing there.

The second wave was just as big as the first—maybe even bigger. From far above my head it began to fall, losing its shape, like a brick wall slowly

10. **READ** ▶ As you read lines 206–247, continue to cite text evidence.

- Circle mentions of silence or soundlessness.
- Underline text where the narrator expresses doubt about what to do.
- In the margin, briefly note the events that happen.

35

crumbling. It was so huge that it no longer looked like a real wave. It was like something from another, far-off world, that just happened to assume the shape of a wave. I readied myself for the moment the darkness would take me. I didn't even close my eyes. I remember hearing my heart pound with incredible clarity.

230 The moment the wave came before me, however, it stopped. All at once it seemed to run out of energy, to lose its forward motion and simply hover there, in space, crumbling in stillness. And in its crest, inside its cruel, transparent tongue, what I saw was K.

Some of you may find this impossible to believe, and if so, I don't blame you. I myself have trouble accepting it even now. I can't explain what I saw any better than you can, but I know it was no illusion, no hallucination. I am telling you as honestly as I can what happened at that moment—what really happened. In the tip of the wave, as if enclosed in some kind of transparent capsule, floated K.'s body, reclining on its side. But that is not all. K. was looking straight at me, smiling. There, right in front of me, so close that I could have reached out and touched him, was my friend, my

240 friend K. who, only moments before, had been swallowed by the wave. And he was smiling at me. Not with an ordinary smile—it was a big, wide-open grin that literally stretched from ear to ear. His cold, frozen eyes were locked on mine. He was no longer the K. I knew. And his right arm was stretched out in my direction, as if he were trying to grab my hand and pull me into that other world where he was now. A little closer, and his hand would have caught mine. But, having missed, K. then smiled at me one more time, his grin wider than ever.

I seem to have lost consciousness at that point. The next thing I knew, I was in bed in my father's clinic. As soon as I awoke the nurse went to call

250 my father, who came running. He took my pulse, studied my pupils, and

11. ◀ **REREAD** Reread lines 206–247. Why do you think the narrator has trouble remembering what happened? How does this affect the believability of his story?

_____

_____

_____

_____

> *One way or another, though, I managed to recover . . . But my life would never be the same again.*

put his hand on my forehead. I tried to move my arm, but couldn't lift it. I was burning with fever, and my mind was clouded. I had been wrestling with a high fever for some time, apparently. "You've been asleep for three days," my father said to me. A neighbor who had seen the whole thing had picked me up and carried me home. They had not been able to find K. I wanted to say something to my father. I *had* to say something to him. But my numb and swollen tongue could not form words. I felt as if some kind of creature had taken up residence in my mouth. My father asked me to tell him my name, but before I could remember what it was, I lost consciousness
260 again, sinking into darkness.

Altogether, I stayed in bed for a week on a liquid diet. I vomited several times, and had bouts of delirium. My father told me afterwards that I was so bad that he had been afraid that I might suffer permanent **neurological** damage from the shock and high fever. One way or another, though, I managed to recover—physically, at least. But my life would never be the same again.

neurological:

12. **READ** ▶ As you read lines 248–289, continue to cite text evidence.

- Underline the example of figurative language in lines 257–258, and analyze it in the margin.
- In the margin, explain the narrator's belief about K.'s death (lines 267–289).

They never found K.'s body. They never found his dog, either. Usually when someone drowned in that area, the body would wash up a few days later on the shore of a small inlet to the east. K.'s body never did. The big

270 waves probably carried it far out to sea—too far for it to reach the shore. It must have sunk to the ocean bottom to be eaten by the fish. The search went on for a very long time, thanks to the cooperation of the local fishermen, but eventually it petered out[1]. Without a body, there was never any funeral. Half crazed, K.'s parents would wander up and down the beach every day, or they would shut themselves up at home, chanting sutras[2].

As great a blow as this had been for them, though, K.'s parents never chided me for having taken their son down to the shore in the midst of a typhoon. They knew how I had always loved and protected K. as if he had been my own little brother. My parents, too, made a point of never

280 mentioning the incident in my presence. But I knew the truth. I knew that I could have saved K. if I had tried. I probably could have run over and dragged him out of the reach of the wave. It would have been close, but as I went over the timing of the events in my memory, it always seemed to me that I could have made it. As I said before, though, overcome with fear, I abandoned him there and saved only myself. It pained me all the more that K.'s parents failed to blame me and that everyone else was so careful never to say anything to me about what had happened. It took me a long time to

---

[1] **petered out:** came to an end.
[2] **sutras:** short Buddhist texts.

---

13. ◀ REREAD Reread lines 261–289. Compare and contrast K.'s parents' reaction to their loss with the narrator's reaction. Support your answer with explicit textual evidence.

_____

_____

_____

_____

_____

_____

recover from the emotional shock. I stayed away from school for weeks. I
hardly ate a thing, and spent each day in bed, staring at the ceiling.

290   K. was always there, lying in the wave tip, grinning at me, his hand
outstretched, beckoning. I couldn't get that picture out of my mind. And
when I managed to sleep, it was there in my dreams—except that, in my
dreams, K. would hop out of his capsule in the wave and grab my wrist to
drag me back inside with him.

And then there was another dream I had. I'm swimming in the ocean.
It's a beautiful summer afternoon, and I'm doing an easy breaststroke far
from shore. The sun is beating down on my back, and the water feels good.
Then, all of a sudden, someone grabs my right leg. I feel an ice-cold grip on
my ankle. It's strong, too strong to shake off. I'm being dragged down under
300   the surface. I see K.'s face there. He has the same huge grin, split from ear to
ear, his eyes locked on mine. I try to scream, but my voice will not come. I
swallow water, and my lungs start to fill.

I wake up in the darkness, screaming, breathless, drenched in sweat.

At the end of the year I pleaded with my parents to let me move to
another town. I couldn't go on living in sight of the beach where K. had
been swept away, and my nightmares wouldn't stop. If I didn't get out of
there, I'd go crazy. My parents understood and made arrangements for me
to live elsewhere. I moved to Nagano Province in January to live with my
father's family in a mountain village near Komoro. I finished elementary
310   school in Nagano and stayed on through junior and senior high school
there. I never went home, even for holidays. My parents came to visit me
now and then.

I live in Nagano to this day. I graduated from a college of engineering in
the City of Nagano and went to work for a precision toolmaker in the area. I
still work for them. I live like anybody else. As you can see, there's nothing
unusual about me. I'm not very sociable, but I have a few friends I go
mountain climbing with. Once I got away from my hometown, I stopped
having nightmares all the time. They remained a part of my life, though.
They would come to me now and then, like debt collectors at the door. It
320   happened when I was on the verge of forgetting. And it was always the same
dream, down to the smallest detail. I would wake up screaming, my sheets
soaked with sweat.

---

14. **READD ▶** As you read lines 290–335, continue to cite text evidence.

- In the margin, describe in your own words the seventh man's dreams.
- Underline text explaining how the seventh man tries to get rid of his
  memories of K.'s death.

That is probably why I never married. I didn't want to wake someone sleeping next to me with my screams in the middle of the night. I've been in love with several women over the years, but I never spent a night with any of them. The terror was in my bones. It was something I could never share with another person.

I stayed away from my hometown for over forty years. I never went near that seashore—or any other. I was afraid that if I did, my dream might
330 happen in reality. I had always enjoyed swimming, but after that day I never even went to swim in a pool. I wouldn't go near deep rivers or lakes. I avoided boats and wouldn't take a plane to go abroad. Despite all these precautions, I couldn't get rid of the image of myself drowning. Like K.'s cold hand, this dark premonition caught hold of my mind and refused to let go.

Then, last spring, I finally revisited the beach where K. had been taken by the wave.

My father had died of cancer the year before, and my brother had sold the old house. In going through the storage shed, he had found a cardboard
340 carton crammed with childhood things of mine, which he sent to me in Nagano. Most of it was useless junk, but there was one bundle of pictures that K. had painted and given to me. My parents had probably put them away for me as a keepsake of K., but the pictures did nothing but reawaken the old terror. They made me feel as if K.'s spirit would spring back to life from them, and so I quickly returned them to their paper wrapping, intending to throw them away. I couldn't make myself do it, though. After several days of indecision, I opened the bundle again and forced myself to take a long, hard look at K.'s watercolors.

15. **◀ REREAD** Reread lines 290–335. Explain how the incident with K. haunts the narrator throughout his life.

_____

_____

_____

_____

16. **READ ▶** As you read lines 336–384, continue to cite text evidence.

• Circle evidence that the narrator has changed.

• In the margin, summarize the sequence of events that occur when the seventh man receives K.'s watercolors.

Most of them were landscapes, pictures of the familiar stretch of ocean
and sand beach and pine woods and the town, and all done with that
special clarity and coloration I knew so well from K.'s hand. They were still
amazingly vivid despite the years, and had been executed with even greater
skill than I recalled. As I leafed through the bundle, I found myself steeped
in warm memories. The deep feelings of the boy K. were there in his
pictures—the way his eyes were opened on the world. The things we did
together, the places we went together began to come back to me with great
intensity. And I realized that his eyes were my eyes, that I myself had looked
upon the world back then with the same lively, unclouded vision as the boy
who had walked by my side.

I made a habit after that of studying one of K.'s pictures at my desk each
day when I got home from work. I could sit there for hours with one
painting. In each I found another of those soft landscapes of childhood that
I had shut out of my memory for so long. I had a sense, whenever I looked at
one of K.'s works, that something was permeating my very flesh.

Perhaps a week had gone by like this when the thought suddenly struck
me one evening: I might have been making a terrible mistake all those
years. As he lay there in the tip of the wave, surely K. had not been looking
at me with hatred or resentment; he had not been trying to take me away
with him. And that terrible grin he had fixed me with: that, too, could have
been an accident of angle or light and shadow, not a conscious act on K.'s
part. He had probably already lost consciousness, or perhaps he had been
giving me a gentle smile of eternal parting. The intense look of hatred I
thought I saw on his face had been nothing but a reflection of the profound
terror that had taken control of me for the moment.

The more I studied K.'s watercolor that evening, the greater the
conviction with which I began to believe these new thoughts of mine. For
no matter how long I continued to look at the picture, I could find nothing
in it but a boy's gentle, innocent spirit.

I went on sitting at my desk for a very long time. There was nothing else
I could do. The sun went down, and the pale darkness of evening began to
envelop the room. Then came the deep silence of night, which seemed to go
on forever. At last, the scales tipped, and dark gave way to dawn. The new
day's sun tinged the sky with pink.

It was then I knew I must go back.

17. ◀ REREAD AND DISCUSS   Reread lines 365–384. In a small group,
discuss why you think the narrator decided he must go back to his
hometown.

I threw a few things in a bag, called the company to say I would not be in, and boarded a train for my old hometown.

I did not find the same quiet, little seaside town that I remembered. An industrial city had sprung up nearby during the rapid development of the Sixties, bringing great changes to the landscape. The one little gift shop by

390 the station had grown into a mall, and the town's only movie theater had been turned into a supermarket. My house was no longer there. It had been demolished some months before, leaving only a scrape on the earth. The trees in the yard had all been cut down, and patches of weeds dotted the black stretch of ground. K.'s old house had disappeared as well, having been replaced by a concrete parking lot full of commuters' cars and vans. Not that I was overcome by **sentiment.** The town had ceased to be mine long before.

I walked down to the shore and climbed the steps of the breakwater. On the other side, as always, the ocean stretched off into the distance,

400 unobstructed, huge, the horizon a single straight line. The shoreline, too, looked the same as it had before: the long beach, the lapping waves, people strolling at the water's edge. The time was after four o'clock, and the soft sun of late afternoon embraced everything below as it began its long, almost meditative descent to the west. I lowered my bag to the sand and sat down next to it in silent appreciation of the gentle seascape. Looking at this scene, it was impossible to imagine that a great typhoon had once raged here, that a massive wave had swallowed my best friend in all the world. There was almost no one left now, surely, who remembered those terrible events. It began to seem as if the whole thing were an illusion that I had dreamed up

410 in vivid detail.

And then I realized that the deep darkness inside me had vanished. Suddenly. As suddenly as it had come. I raised myself from the sand, and, without bothering to take off my shoes or roll up my cuffs, walked into the surf and let the waves lap at my ankles.

sentiment:

18. **READ ▶** As you read lines 385–449, continue to cite evidence.

Continue to circle text that shows the narrator has changed.

Almost in **reconciliation,** it seemed, the same waves that had washed up on the beach when I was a boy were now fondly washing my feet, soaking black my shoes and pant cuffs. There would be one slow-moving wave, then a long pause, and then another wave would come and go. The people passing by gave me odd looks, but I didn't care.

reconciliation:

420   I looked up at the sky. A few grey cotton chunks of cloud hung there, motionless. They seemed to be there for me, though I'm not sure why I felt that way. I remembered having looked up at the sky like this in search of the "eye" of the typhoon. And then, inside me, the axis of time gave one great heave. Forty long years collapsed like a dilapidated house, mixing old time and new time together in a single swirling mass. All sounds faded, and the light around me shuddered. I lost my balance and fell into the waves. My heart throbbed at the back of my throat, and my arms and legs lost all sensation. I lay that way for a long time, face in the water, unable to stand. But I was not afraid. No, not at all. There was no longer anything for me to
430   fear. Those days were gone.

I stopped having my terrible nightmares. I no longer wake up screaming in the middle of the night. And I am trying now to start life over again. No, I know it's probably too late to start again. I may not have much time left to live. But even if it comes too late, I am grateful that, in the end, I was able to attain a kind of salvation, to effect some sort of recovery. Yes, grateful: I could have come to the end of my life unsaved, still screaming in the dark, afraid.

The seventh man fell silent and turned his gaze upon each of the others. No one spoke or moved or even seemed to breathe. All were waiting for the rest of his story. Outside, the wind had fallen, and nothing stirred. The seventh man brought his hand to his collar once again, as if in search for words.

"They tell us that the only thing we have to fear is fear itself; but I don't believe that," he said. Then, a moment later, he added: "Oh, the fear is there, all right. It comes to us in many different forms, at different times, and overwhelms us. But the most frightening thing we can do at such times is to turn our backs on it, to close our eyes. For then we take the most precious thing inside us and surrender it to something else. In my case, that something was the wave."

19. **◀ REREAD** Reread lines 438–449. What does the narrator think is more frightening than fear itself?

_____

_____

_____

SHORT RESPONSE

Cite Text Evidence What theme, or central idea, about fear does Murakami explore in "The Seventh Man." How does his use of figurative language help him advance his theme? Review your reading notes, and be sure to **cite evidence** from the story in your response.

_____

_____

_____

_____

_____

_____

_____

_____

Responses to Change

COLLECTION 3

Responses to Change

"When the wind of change blows, some build walls while others build windmills."

—Chinese proverb

The Starry Night

PAINTING	
The Starry Night	**Vincent van Gogh**

POEM	
The Starry Night	**Anne Sexton**

SCIENCE WRITING
Life After People   **Dolores Vasquez**

Background *In June 1889,* **Vincent van Gogh** *painted* The Starry Night *during a stay at an asylum in Saint-Remy, in southern France. The painting is of the view outside of his window, although the depiction of the village comes partly from van Gogh's imagination. The church spire resembles of the architecture of the Netherlands, van Gogh's home.* The Starry Night *has been part of the permanent collection of the Museum of Modern Art in New York City since 1941. Almost a century later, Anne Sexton wrote her poem "The Starry Night" (based on van Gogh's painting). The poem opens with a quote from a letter from van Gogh to his brother Theo.*

The Starry Night

The Starry Night (painting) . . . . Vincent van Gogh

The Starry Night (poem) . . . . Anne Sexton

Vincent van Gogh *(1853–1890) was a Dutch impressionist artist. His first profession was as an art dealer, but he soon turned to making his own art. Between November 1881 and July 1890, van Gogh painted almost 900 paintings. He sold only one painting in the course of his life, but became one of the most famous and influential artists in history. Van Gogh suffered from mental illness and anxiety throughout his life. At the age of 37, he died from a gunshot wound that most think was self-inflicted, although a gun was never found.*

Anne Sexton *(1928–1974) was an American poet born in Massachusetts. Married at 20, she worked for a time as a fashion model, gave birth to two children, and then, at age twenty-eight, began writing poetry. Known for her personal, confessional style, Sexton won the Pulitzer Prize for poetry in 1967. Like van Gogh, she spent time in several mental hospitals, and her poems often display a storm of emotions. Describing her own work, Sexton said, "Poetry should almost hurt."*

1. **READ ▶** As you view the painting,

   • write notes in the margin about what your eyes are drawn to first in the painting.
   • locate the following images: cypress trees, stars, the moon, the village.

The Starry Night
by Vincent Van Gogh

The Starry Night
Vincent van Gogh (Dutch, 1853–1890)

Saint Rémy, June 1889. Oil on canvas, 29 x 36 1/4" (73.7 x 92.1 cm).
Acquired through the Lillie P. Bliss Bequest

2. **◀ REREAD** Study the painting again. Then, consider this quote from van Gogh to his brother Theo: "Looking at the stars always makes me dream. Why, I ask myself, shouldn't the shining dots of the sky be as accessible as the black dots on the map of France?" In what ways does van Gogh make the stars accessible? In what ways do the stars contrast with the village?

_____

_____

_____

_____

3. **READ ▶** As you read the poem, collect and cite text evidence.

- Underline imagery that relates to the stars and moon.
- Circle language that refers to the town.
- In the margin, make an inference about the night based on the language Sexton uses.

The Starry Night
by Anne Sexton

That does not keep me from having a terrible need of—I shall
say the word—religion. Then I go out at night to paint the stars.
—Vincent Van Gogh in a letter to his brother

The town does not exist
5   except where one black-haired tree slips
up like a drowned woman into the hot sky.
The town is silent. The night boils with eleven stars.
Oh starry starry night! This is how
I want to die.

10 It moves. They are all alive.
Even the moon bulges in its orange irons
to push children, like a god, from its eye.
The old unseen serpent swallows up the stars.
Oh starry starry night! This is how
15 I want to die:

into that rushing beast of the night.
sucked up by that great dragon, to split
from my life with no flag,
no belly,
20 no cry.

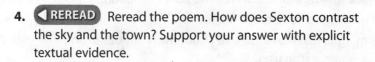

4. **◀ REREAD**   Reread the poem. How does Sexton contrast
the sky and the town? Support your answer with explicit
textual evidence.

_____

_____

_____

_____

_____

SHORT RESPONSE

Cite Text Evidence   In what ways does Sexton's poem evoke the
painting? What parts of the painting does she emphasize? Review your
reading notes, and be sure to **cite text evidence** from the poem and the
painting in your response.

_____

_____

_____

_____

_____

_____

_____

_____

_____

_____

Background *Human beings are a fairly recent arrival on Earth. In fact, many archaeologists estimate that Homo sapiens have been here for about 200,000 years, a fraction of the lifetime of Earth—approximately 4.6 billion years. In those 200,000 years, human beings have left their mark on the planet. But what would happen if we suddenly disappeared? The article below, accompanied by photographs from HISTORY's television show "Life After People," illustrates what a planet without people might look like.*

Life After People

Article by Dolores Vasquez

CLOSE READ
Notes

1. **READD ▶** As you read lines 1–12, begin to collect and cite text evidence.

   • Circle the question at the beginning of the article.
   • In the margin, paraphrase the central idea in lines 2–4, and underline the details that support it.
   • In the margin, explain the central idea in lines 5–12.

What would the world be like if people suddenly disappeared? Imagine the immediate consequences: wrecks from driverless cars and planes; saucepans boiling over; startled dogs dragging their leashes down deserted streets. But what happens later?

Without people to fuel them, power plants stop providing electricity— within hours. We use electricity to make toast and to power TVs and computers, but the absence of electric energy has huge effects on an Earth void of human population. Without electricity, gas tanks are not kept cold; gases such as chlorine and natural gas heat up and escape the tanks into the air. Animals die from the freed chlorine fumes, and the natural gas causes explosions and uncontrolled fires. Within days, treatment facilities are at a standstill and sewage begins to poison rivers and lakes.

10

After one year, plants and shrubs begin to overrun the highway system in Los Angeles.

By the end of the first week, pets that have run out of food in their homes must escape and try to survive in the new environment. The larger dogs form packs and prey on smaller animals. Dairy cattle die of thirst in their pens, and their bodies may provide food for scavenging dogs. Cows that were raised as food, however, will eventually establish huge herds on the plains, reinterpreting the lifestyle of the buffalo in the 1800s. Zoo animals that had been restrained by electric fences wander city streets. But
20 within weeks, many animals leave the cities to the mice, rats, and squirrels.

Meanwhile, at nuclear power plants, the cooling ponds for spent fuel rods get hotter and hotter. Soon the water boils away, and the rods cause fires and release radiation into the air, where it is carried by the wind. Plants and animals in affected areas die.

2. **◀ REREAD** Reread lines 1–12. Then, write a summary of the text so far, including essential supporting details.

_____

_____

_____

_____

3. **READ ▶** As you read lines 13–24, continue to cite textual evidence.

• Circle time-order words or phrases that introduce chronological events.

• In the margin, explain how the author develops her ideas and shows a relationship between events.

© Houghton Mifflin Harcourt Publishing Company • Image Credits: ©Flight 33 Productions LLC

After 200 years of neglect, the rusted skeleton of the Chrysler Building in New York finally collapses.

After several months, the radiation in the air is no longer a danger, and those animals that have survived begin to follow their new lives. And by the end of a year, rains have washed the radioactive pollution from the surface of the land.

Over the next fifteen years, the roads get overgrown and cracked. Yards 30 and gardens grow wild, and some animals make their homes in urban areas. Packs of dogs still roam the cities and countryside. Some sports stadiums become giant bat caves. As time passes, the roofs of buildings cave in, and trees and other plants grow in what used to be the indoors. Windows fall, paint is eroded, and concrete cracks. Plants begin to blanket the cities. Pet parrots—whose life span can be 60 years—may form flocks, still speaking the words they had been taught by their human owners.

4. **◀ REREAD** Reread lines 13–24. List several cause-and-effect relationships to show a connection between events.

_____

_____

_____

_____

5. **READ ▶** As you read lines 25–48, continue to cite textual evidence.

- Circle each time-order word or phrase that introduces an event in chronological order.
- In the margin, explain how the author develops her ideas and shows a relationship among events.

Between 50 and 100 years after the disappearance of human beings, skyscrapers begin to tumble. Bridges fall. The hulks of cars and buses start to disintegrate. The packs of dogs have reverted to their origins—they are

40   no longer German shepherds and Dobermans, but a single species more like a wolf. In cooler climates, the mighty cockroach meets its end; it cannot survive in unheated buildings.

After 250 years, the Statue of Liberty loses its torch. Old stone buildings have outlasted the toppled glass skyscrapers, especially as acid rain is no longer eroding them. But they are hidden under a mass of vegetation. Forests cover the eastern states, and over the next 250 years they return almost to the way they were ten thousand years ago.

It looks as though we had never been here.

6.   **◄ REREAD**   Reread lines 37–42. Determine the central ideas of this paragraph, and note it in the margin.

SHORT RESPONSE

Cite Text Evidence   Use the central idea of the article and its development over the course of the article to write an objective summary of the text. Review your reading notes and **cite text evidence** in your response.

_____

_____

_____

_____

_____

_____

_____

_____

_____

_____

How We See Things

How We See Things

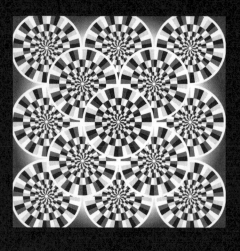

"The question is not what you look at, but what you see."

—Henry David Thoreau

Background *Sometimes it's best to read more than one poem by an author to get a feel for his or her style. Read these poems more than once. Who knows? "The Trouble with Poetry" might just inspire you to write your own poem, using ideas from the other poems that you have read. "Today" might force you to look out the window.*

Poems by

Billy Collins

Billy Collins *has been called "the most popular poet in America" for his witty, and often funny poems. He served two terms as U.S. Poet Laureate, during which time he created a poetry program called* Poetry 180 *to get more high school students to read poetry each day during the 180-day school year.*

Speaking about his writing process, Collins has said: "I have one reader in mind, someone who is in the room with me, and who I'm talking to, and I want to make sure I don't talk too fast, or too glibly. Usually I try to create a hospitable tone at the beginning of a poem. Stepping from the title to the first lines is like stepping into a canoe. A lot of things can go wrong."

1. **READ ▶** As you read lines 1–27 of "The Trouble with Poetry," begin to collect and cite evidence.

   - Underline repeating phrases.
   - Circle what "the trouble with poetry" is.
   - In the margin, paraphrase lines 1–16.

The Trouble with Poetry

The trouble with poetry, I realized
as I walked along a beach one night—
cold Florida sand under my bare feet,
a show of stars in the sky—

5   the trouble with poetry is
that it encourages the writing of more poetry,
more guppies crowding the fish tank,
more baby rabbits
hopping out of their mothers into the dewy grass.

10   And how will it ever end?
unless the day finally arrives
when we have compared everything in the world
to everything else in the world,

and there is nothing left to do
15   but quietly close our notebooks
and sit with our hands folded on our desks.

Poetry fills me with joy
and I rise like a feather in the wind.
Poetry fills me with sorrow
20   and I sink like a chain flung from a bridge.

But mostly poetry fills me
with the urge to write poetry,
to sit in the dark and wait for a little flame
to appear at the tip of my pencil.

25 And along with that, the longing to steal,
to break into the poems of others
with a flashlight and a ski mask.

And what an unmerry band of thieves we are,
cut-purses, common shoplifters,
30 I thought to myself
as a cold wave swirled around my feet
and the lighthouse moved its megaphone over the sea,
which is an image I stole directly
from Lawrence Ferlinghetti[1]—
35 to be perfectly honest for a moment—

the bicycling poet of San Francisco
whose little amusement park of a book
I carried in a side pocket of my uniform
up and down the treacherous halls of high school.

_____

[1] **Lawrence Ferlinghetti:** American poet and founder of City Lights Bookstore in San
Francisco. His poem "To the Oracle at Delphi" contains the lines "as a lighthouse moves
its megaphone / over the sea" which Collins references here.

2. **◄ REREAD** Reread lines 1–27. What does the poet mean by "the
trouble with poetry"? Cite evidence from the poem.

_____

_____

_____

_____

_____

3. **READ ▷** As you read lines 28–39, continue to cite textual evidence.

• In the margin, explain how many sentences the poet uses in these lines,
and what effect that has on the reader.

• Underline the lines that explain how he uses another poet's words and
where he first encountered his work.

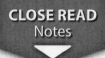

> " *Poetry fills me with joy . . .*
> *Poetry fills me with sorrow . . .* "

---

4. ◀ **REREAD** Reread lines 28–39. Explain what Collins says about the poet Lawrence Ferlinghetti.

_____

_____

_____

_____

SHORT RESPONSE

Cite Text Evidence   In your own words, write a summary of "The Trouble with Poetry." Then, think about what you left out. Which lines or phrases are the most difficult to say in other words? **Cite text evidence** in your response.

_____

_____

_____

_____

_____

_____

_____

_____

_____

1. **READ ▷** As you read lines 1–18 of "Today," begin to collect evidence.

- Underline actions that a spring day might inspire.
- Write in the margin where the speaker is, and circle the detail(s) that support your conclusion.
- Circle the punctuation at the end of each line.

Today

If ever there were a spring day so perfect,
so uplifted by a warm **intermittent** breeze

that it made you want to throw
open all the windows in the house

5   and unlatch the door to the canary's cage,
indeed, rip the little door from its jamb,

a day when the cool brick paths
and the garden bursting with peonies

seemed so **etched** in sunlight
10 that you felt like taking

a hammer to the glass paperweight
on the living room end table,

releasing the inhabitants
from their snow-covered cottage

15 so they could walk out,
holding hands and squinting

into this larger dome of blue and white,
well, today is just that kind of day.

intermittent:

etched:

Billy Collins reads his poetry at the grand opening of Poets House in New York City, 2009.

2. **◀ REREAD** Reread the poem. How does the poem's structure of run-on lines within and between the couplets echo the speaker's feelings?

_____

_____

_____

_____

SHORT RESPONSE

Cite Text Evidence   How is the speaker like the canary and the paperweight's inhabitants? Review your reading notes, and be sure to **cite evidence** from the text in your response.

_____

_____

_____

_____

_____

_____

_____

_____

Background *Everyone has noticed that sometimes time seems to fly and sometimes it seems to crawl. Our perception of time is a result of brain processes that have to do with memory and attention. Really, it isn't time that we perceive, but changes or events in time. British writer, broadcaster, and lecturer Claudia Hammond wrote the book* Time Warped *to examine "the way we actively construct this experience of time in our minds." Find out more in this book review.*

Every Second Counts

Book Review by Matilda Battersby

1. **READL ▷** As you read lines 1–15, begin to cite evidence.

- Underline three commonly used sayings in lines 1–9.
- In the margin, explain what Battersby means when she says "time is elastic" in line 6.
- Circle the question she asks in lines 10–15.

CLOSE READ
Notes

Time is of the essence. Time heals all wounds. Time flies when you're having fun . . . Such time-based **platitudes** are neverending. In fact, time is the most-used noun in the English language, so concerned are we by our position in it, our grasp of it—and its power over us.

platitude:

The platitudes exist because they represent broad, if scientifically unproven, notions that time is elastic. Time does seem to fly by when we're having fun. Likewise, it stretches out ad infinitum when we're willing it to zip past and deliver us with birthdays, Christmas Day or that longed-for holiday.

10 But how often do we examine the many nuances of our relationship with time? It is a construct, after all. If I were a member of the Amazon's Amondawa tribe I would have no word for time, no clocks and no calendar to chart months or years passing. But that doesn't mean my past, present or future would be fundamentally any different. Yet we rely on (and obsess about) timekeeping, time-saving and the rate at which we gobble it up.

There have been endless studies into time perception, whether or not time ticks away faster at altitude or whether there is any physical basis for the universal conclusion that time moves more slowly when we are children and speeds up as we grow older. Nobody knows the amount of time they will live in their lives and yet we claim time as our own, demand more, and feel cheated when we lose it.

Claudia Hammond, the psychology lecturer, broadcaster, and writer, has a better understanding than most of the ways that our perspectives on time can be morphed, manipulated and played with.

Her new book, *Time Warped*, examines the myriad ways that time seems to change gear. She also looks at our sense of time aesthetically and discovered that people visualize time in offbeat ways. Some see it as curling around like a Slinky or a roll of wallpaper; others may view days of the week as rectangles. To some, Monday is the color red (though it is yellow to me).

The puzzles of time, the tricks it plays and the ways we unconsciously amend our relationship with it are explored in detail by Hammond. She has come up with the "holiday paradox," a description of the way that when we're relaxing on holiday, we feel that time cannot go faster. It whizzes by as we pack it full of new experiences. But when we look back afterwards, it feels as if we've been away for ages.

Here she explains (or disproves) other mysteries of time.

Time is determined by the body's circadian rhythms FALSE

The circadian rhythms[1] affect only our 24-hour day/night cycle. They have nothing else to do with our perception of time from moment to moment. It's a myth that they affect time. We do, however, run an automatic body clock. This can go out of sync, which is known as "free running." This is common particularly in blind people, who are isolated

---

[1] **circadian rhythm:** a biological rhythmic activity cycle taking place within the span of a 24-hour day.

---

2. **◀ REREAD**   Reread lines 1–9. What is the central idea in these lines? What details support this idea?

_____

_____

_____

3. **READ ▷**   As you read lines 16–35, continue to cite evidence.

• Underline the key points the author makes.
• Summarize lines 22–35 in the margin.

© Houghton Mifflin Harcourt Publishing Company

from environmental time cues. In most of us, however, the circadian oscillations correct themselves using daylight.

Time speeds up as we get older FALSE

People think that time speeds up when we get older. But it's not true that time at any one moment (ie second by second) gets faster. It's our experiences over days, weeks, months and years that seem to condense. There's no biological basis for the sensation that it speeds up. It's simply to
50 do with our judgments on time **prospectively** and **retrospectively**. Looking back, time seems to go faster, but it can also be strangely elastic.

Time is money TRUE

Social psychologist Robert Levine measured three things in 31 countries around the world to determine the tempo of life: the time taken to buy a stamp, average walking speed of pedestrians during rush hour, and the accuracy of clocks on the walls of banks. It followed that places such as London and New York had the fastest times and that there was a correlation (though this was pre-recession) between the pace of life and gross domestic product. This suggests a connection between time and money, though it
60 isn't known which came first—the culture of rushing around or the buoyant economy.

We can mentally time-travel TRUE

We are the one animal able completely, at will, to throw ourselves backwards into the past or forwards into the future. The ability to conceive events that haven't happened yet is a crucial basis for our imagination. The reason our memories are so bad and let us down actually allows us mentally to time-travel into the future. The unreliability of memory is actually an indication of this sophistication. The mind uses our sense of space and memories to create a sense of the future. Amnesia sufferers lose the ability
70 to imagine the future, as well as their ability to recall who they are or what's happened to them.

Time feels slower when you want something done fast TRUE

Psychologists Chen-Bo Zhong and Sanford DeVoe conducted experiments that revealed that exposure to fast food, both visual symbols and actual food, increases feelings of impatience. We associate fast food with being in a hurry or a rush. This anxiety makes us feel time is going

---

4. **◄ REREAD AND DISCUSS** Reread lines 30–35. With a small group, discuss what Hammond means by the "holiday paradox."

5. **READ ▶** Read lines 36–85. Circle the boldfaced headings and underline the key points in each paragraph.

more slowly. Research shows people felt they had been waiting for far longer than they actually had.

Our sense of time can be affected by biological conditions TRUE

80   A high temperature (a fever, not just wearing too many jumpers[2]) makes our perception of time change so it feels slower. American psychologist Hudson Hoagland's wife was lying in bed with bad flu and she allowed him to conduct time tests on her. Hoagland asked her to say when a minute had passed 30 times over a day. When her temperature reached 103°F, she felt a minute was up after just 34 seconds.

---

[2] **jumpers:** British term for sweaters.

6. ◀ REREAD   Reread lines 36–85. What structure does the author use to discuss key points? In what way are they introduced and developed?

_____

_____

_____

_____

_____

SHORT RESPONSE

Cite Text Evidence   Write an objective summary of this book review. Analyze the way in which key points are introduced and developed. **Cite evidence** from the text in your response.

_____

_____

_____

_____

_____

_____

_____

Background *The whale shark truly is a "whale of a shark." It measures up to 59 feet long, weighs up to 15 tons, and may live to be 60–100 years old. The world's largest shark and the largest fish, the whale shark has an enormous mouth, which can be 4 feet wide. Its 300 rows of tiny teeth, however, are of little use since it is a filter feeder that feeds its colossal appetite by filtering small food from the water with its gills while it swims. Read the following article to learn more about how the whale shark uses math to move.*

Whale Sharks Use Geometry to Avoid Sinking

Science Writing from *ScienceDaily*

CLOSE READ
Notes

1. **READ ▶** As you read lines 1–12, begin to collect and cite text evidence.

   • Underline the text that describes the topic of the selection.
   • Circle the text that explains why movement is more complex for birds and marine animals.
   • In the margin, explain what this article will be about.

They are the largest fish species in the ocean, but the majestic gliding motion of the whale shark is, scientists argue, an astonishing feat of mathematics and energy conservation. In new research published November 25, 2010 in the British Ecological Society's journal *Functional Ecology* marine scientists reveal how these massive sharks use geometry to enhance their natural negative buoyancy[1] and stay afloat.

For most animals movement is crucial for survival, both for finding food and for evading predators. However, movement costs substantial amounts of energy and while this is true of land-based animals it is even 10 more complex for birds and marine animals which travel in three dimensions. Unsurprisingly this has a profound impact on their movement patterns.

---

[1] **negative buoyancy:** the property of an animal or object that causes it to sink, rather than float, in water.

"The key factor for animal movement is travel speed, which governs how much energy an animal uses, the distance it will travel and how often resources are encountered," said lead author Adrian Gleiss from Swansea University. "However, oceanic animals not only have to consider their travel speed, but also how vertical movement will affect their energy expenditure, which changes the whole perspective."

20   For the past four years, Adrian Gleiss and Rory Wilson, from Swansea University, worked with Brad Norman from ECOcean Inc. to lead an international team to investigate the movements of whale sharks, Rhincodon typus, at Ningaloo Reef in Western Australia. They attached animal-borne motion sensors, accelerometers,[2] to the free-swimming whale sharks to measure their swimming activity and vertical movement, which allowed them to quantify the energetic cost of vertical movement.

----

[2] **accelerometer:** a device that measures acceleration forces, allowing a scientist to determine the vertical angle at which it is moving.

2. ◀ **REREAD**   Reread lines 7–12. Why would having negative buoyancy require a whale shark to use more energy to move through the ocean?

_____

_____

_____

3. **READ** ▷   Read lines 13–25 and continue to cite text evidence.

• Underline the key ideas in these lines.
• In the margin, explain the meaning of lines 13–18 in your own words.

The team's data revealed that whale sharks are able to glide without investing energy into movement when descending, but they had to beat their tails when they ascended. This occurs because sharks, unlike many fish, have negative buoyancy.

30   Also, the steeper the sharks ascended, the harder they had to beat their tail and the more energy they had to invest. The whale sharks displayed two broad movement modes, one consisting of shallow ascent angles, which minimize the energetic cost of moving in the horizontal while a second characteristic of steeper ascent angles, optimized the energetic cost of vertical movement.

4. **◀ REREAD**   Reread lines 19–25. What does the "quantify the energetic cost of vertical movement" mean?

_____

_____

_____

_____

_____

5. **READ ▶**   As you read lines 26–40, continue to cite textual evidence.

• Underline the key points in each paragraph.

• In the margin of lines 26–29, explain the claim in your own words.

"These results demonstrate how geometry plays a crucial role in movement strategies for animals moving in 3-dimensions," concluded Gleiss. "This use of negative buoyancy may play a large part in oceanic sharks being able to locate and travel between scarce and unpredictable
40 food sources efficiently."

6. ◀ REREAD   Reread lines 30–40. In your own words, explain the two kinds of movements the whale sharks displayed.

_____

_____

_____

SHORT RESPONSE

Cite Text Evidence   What claim does this article make about whale sharks? How is this claim supported? **Cite evidence from the text** in your explanation.

_____

_____

_____

_____

_____

_____

_____

_____

_____

_____

Absolute Power

Absolute Power

"Be bloody, bold, and resolute; laugh to scorn the power of man."

—*Macbeth*, Act IV, Scene 1

DRAMA

from The Tragedy of Macbeth
Act I

William Shakespeare

Background Macbeth *is a tragedy: a kind of play in which human actions have their own inevitable consequences, in which the characters' bad deeds, errors, and crimes are never forgiven or rectified. In* **William Shakespeare's** *tragedies the main character, or tragic hero, is usually a high-ranking person distinguished by bravery and intelligence. The hero's character also includes a fatal weakness or tragic flaw that permits an ill-judged action to lead remorselessly to catastrophe.*

from
The Tragedy of
Macbeth

Drama by William Shakespeare

CLOSE READ
Notes

THE TIME: The 11th century   **THE PLACE:** Scotland and England

CHARACTERS

Duncan, King of Scotland

His Sons
    Malcolm
    Donalbain

Noblemen of Scotland
    Macbeth
    Banquo
    Lennox
    Ross
    Angus

Lady Macbeth
Three Witches
Captain
Messenger
Attendants

1. **READ ▶** As you read Scene 1, and Scene 2 lines 1–24, begin to collect and cite text evidence.

   - In the margin, explain where the witches plan to meet again, and why.
   - Underline the witches' references to threatening aspects of nature.
   - In the margin, explain the characteristics Macbeth shows in battle.

The play opens in a wild and lonely place in medieval Scotland. The king of Scotland, Duncan, along with his sons Malcolm and Donalbain, is engaged in a war against Scottish rebels and then faces an attack by the king of Norway. However, the first characters Shakespeare introduces are supernatural beings—witches who seem able to foretell the future.

ACT I

Scene 1 • *An open place in Scotland.*

[*Thunder and lightning. Enter three* Witches.]

First Witch. When shall we three meet again?
In thunder, lightning, or in rain?

Second Witch. When the hurly-burly's done,
When the battle's lost and won.

5   **Third Witch.** That will be ere the set of sun.

First Witch. Where the place?

Second Witch.   Upon the heath.

Third Witch. There to meet with Macbeth.

First Witch. I come, Graymalkin.

Second Witch. Paddock[1] calls.

Third Witch.   Anon.[2]

10   **All.** Fair is foul, and foul is fair,
Hover through the fog and filthy air.

[*They exit.*]

---

[1] **Graymalkin . . . Paddock:** two demons in the form of a cat and a toad.
[2] **anon:** soon.

2. **◀ REREAD** Reread Scene 1. Describe the mood or atmosphere created by the witches and the weather.

_____

_____

_____

Scene 2 • *King Duncan's camp near the battlefield.*

[*Alarum within.*[3] *Enter* King Duncan, Malcolm, Donalbain, Lennox, *with*
Attendants, *meeting a bleeding* Captain.]

Duncan. What bloody man is that? He can report,
As seemeth by his plight, of the revolt
The newest state.

Malcolm.   This is the sergeant
Who, like a good and hardy soldier, fought

5   'Gainst my captivity.[4]—Hail, brave friend!
Say to the King the knowledge of the broil[5]
As thou didst leave it.

Captain.   Doubtful it stood,
As two spent swimmers that do cling together
And choke their art.[6] The merciless Macdonwald

10 (Worthy to be a rebel, for to that
The multiplying villainies of nature
Do swarm upon him) from the Western Isles
Of kerns and gallowglasses[7] is supplied;
And Fortune, on his damnèd quarrel smiling,

15 Showed like a rebel's whore. But all's too weak;
For brave Macbeth (well he deserves that name),
Disdaining Fortune, with his brandished steel,
Which smoked with bloody execution,
Like valor's **minion**, carved out his passage   minion:

20 Till he faced the slave;

---

[3] **Alarum within:** the sound of a trumpet offstage, signaling soldiers to arm themselves.
[4] **'Gainst my captivity:** to save me from capture.
[5] **broil:** battle.
[6] **choke their art:** drown each other.
[7] **kerns and gallowglasses:** foot soldiers and armed horsemen.

3. (READ ▶) As you read Scene 2, lines 25–70, continue to cite textual
   evidence.

   • Circle the name of the captain who fights alongside Macbeth. Then, circle
     the lines that describe the two men in battle.

   • In the margin, explain the animal analogies (line 35).

   • In the margin, summarize Ross's report to Duncan (lines 50–60).

> "Go, pronounce his present death, And with his former title greet Macbeth."

Which ne'er shook hands, nor bade farewell to him,
Till he unseamed him from the nave to th' chops,[8]
And fixed his head upon our battlements.

Duncan. O valiant cousin, worthy gentleman!

25 **Captain.** As whence the sun 'gins his reflection
Shipwracking storms and direful thunders break,
So from that spring whence comfort seemed to come
Discomfort swells. Mark, King of Scotland, mark:
No sooner justice had, with valor armed,

30 Compelled these skipping kerns to trust their heels,
But the Norweyan lord, surveying vantage,
With furbished arms and new supplies of men,
Began a fresh assault.

Duncan. Dismayed not this our captains, Macbeth and Banquo?

35 **Captain.** Yes, as sparrows eagles, or the hare the lion.
If I say sooth, I must report they were
As cannons overcharged with double cracks,
So they doubly redoubled strokes upon the foe.
Except they meant to bathe in reeking wounds

40 Or memorize another Golgotha,[9]
I cannot tell—
But I am faint. My gashes cry for help.

Duncan. So well thy words become thee as thy wounds:
They smack of honor both.—Go, get him surgeons.

[*The* Captain *is led off by* Attendants.]

[*Enter* Ross *and* Angus.]

45 Who comes here?

Malcolm. The worthy Thane[10] of Ross.

Lennox. What a haste looks through his eyes!
So should he look that seems to speak things strange.

Ross. God save the King.

---

[8] **unseamed him from the nave to th' chops:** split him open from navel to jaw.

[9] **memorize another Golgotha:** make the battlefield as famous as Golgotha, the site of Christ's crucifixion.

[10] **Thane:** a rank of Scottish nobleman.

© Houghton Mifflin Harcourt Publishing Company • Image Credits: ©Stephanie Frey/Shutterstock

Duncan. Whence cam'st thou, worthy thane?

50 **Ross.** From Fife, great king,

Where the Norweyan banners flout the sky

And fan our people cold.

Norway himself, with terrible numbers,

Assisted by that most disloyal traitor,

55 The Thane of Cawdor, began a dismal conflict,

Till that Bellona's bridegroom,[11] lapped in proof,

Confronted him with self-comparisons,[12]

Point against point, rebellious arm 'gainst arm,

Curbing his lavish spirit. And to conclude,

60 The victory fell on us.

Duncan.   Great happiness!

Ross. That now Sweno,

The Norways' king, craves composition.[13]

Nor would we deign him burial of his men

Till he disbursèd at Saint Colme's Inch

65 Ten thousand dollars to our general use.

Duncan. No more that Thane of Cawdor shall deceive

Our bosom interest. Go, pronounce his present death,

And with his former title greet Macbeth.

Ross. I'll see it done.

70 **Duncan.** What he hath lost, noble Macbeth hath won.

[*They exit.*]

---

[11] **Bellona's bridegroom:** Macbeth is referred to as the groom of Bellona, the Roman goddess of war.

[12] **self-comparisons:** equal deeds.

[13] **craves composition:** wants a treaty.

---

4. **◀ REREAD** Reread Scene 2, lines 66–70. Who is punished, and who is rewarded? What is the punishment, and what is the reward? Support your answer with explicit textual evidence.

_____

_____

_____

_____

_____

Scene 3 • *A bleak place near the battlefield.*

[*Thunder. Enter the three* Witches.]

First Witch. Where hast thou been, sister?

Second Witch. Killing swine.

Third Witch. Sister, where thou?

First Witch. A sailor's wife had chestnuts in her lap

5 And munched and munched and munched. "Give me," quoth I.

"Aroint thee,[14] witch," the rump-fed runnion[15] cries.

Her husband's to Aleppo gone, master o' th' *Tiger*;

But in a sieve I'll thither sail

And, like a rat without a tail,

10 I'll do, I'll do, and I'll do.

Second Witch. I'll give thee a wind.

First Witch. Th' art kind.

Third Witch. And I another.

First Witch. I myself have all the other,

15 And the very ports they blow,

All the quarters that they know

I' th' shipman's card.[16]

I'll drain him dry as hay.

Sleep shall neither night nor day

20 Hang upon his penthouse lid.

He shall live a man forbid.

Weary sev'nnights,[17] nine times nine,

Shall he dwindle, peak, and pine.

Though his bark cannot be lost,

25 Yet it shall be tempest-tossed.

---

[14] **Aroint thee:** Go away.

[15] **rump-fed runion:** fat-bottomed, ugly creature.

[16] **card:** compass.

[17] **sev'nnights:** weeks.

---

5. **READ ▶** As you read Scene 3, lines 1–37, continue to cite textual evidence.

• Underline examples of the witches' malicious behavior or plans for such behavior.

• In the margin, explain the extent of the witches' power and the way in which they use it (lines 8–25).

Look what I have.

Second Witch. Show me, show me.

First Witch. Here I have a pilot's thumb,

Wracked as homeward he did come.

[*Drum within*]

30   **Third Witch.** A drum, a drum!

Macbeth doth come.

All. [*Dancing in a circle*] The Weïrd[18] Sisters, hand in hand,

Posters[19] of the sea and land,

Thus do go about, about,

35   Thrice to thine, and thrice to mine

And thrice again, to make up nine.

Peace, the charm's wound up.

[*Enter* Macbeth *and* Banquo.]

Macbeth. So foul and fair a day I have not seen.

Banquo. How far is 't called to Forres?—What are these,

40   So withered, and so wild in their attire,

That look not like th' inhabitants o' th' earth

And yet are on 't?—Live you? Or are you aught

That man may question? You seem to understand me

By each at once her choppy finger laying

---

[18] **Weïrd:** related to the Old English word *wyrd* (fate or personal destiny); these "weïrd sisters" manipulate fate.

[19] **posters:** quick riders.

6. **◀ REREAD** Reread Scene 3, lines 8–25. *Fate* is a theme in *Macbeth*. If the witches can foresee the fate of others, what effect or influence do you think they will have on the outcome of the play?

_____

_____

_____

7. **READ ▶** As you read Scene 3, lines 38–88, continue to cite textual evidence.

   • Underline the witches' predictions for Macbeth and Banquo, and restate them in the margin.

   • In the margin, explain why Macbeth disbelieves the witches at first (lines 71–75).

> # So foul and fair a day I have not seen.

45   Upon her skinny lips. You should be women,

And yet your beards forbid me to interpret

That you are so.

Macbeth.   Speak, if you can. What are you?

First Witch. All hail, Macbeth! Hail to thee, Thane of Glamis!

Second Witch. All hail, Macbeth! Hail to thee, Thane of Cawdor!

50   **Third Witch.** All hail, Macbeth, that shalt be king hereafter!

Banquo. Good sir, why do you start and seem to fear

Things that do sound so fair? I' th' name of truth,

fantastical: Are you **fantastical**, or that indeed

Which outwardly you show? My noble partner

55   You greet with present grace and great prediction

Of noble having and of royal hope,

rapt: That he seems **rapt** withal. To me you speak not.

If you can look into the seeds of time

And say which grain will grow and which will not,

60   Speak, then, to me, who neither beg nor fear

Your favors nor your hate.

First Witch. Hail!

Second Witch. Hail!

Third Witch. Hail!

65   **First Witch.** Lesser than Macbeth and greater.

Second Witch. Not so happy,[20] yet much happier.

Third Witch. Thou shalt get[21] kings, though thou be none.

So all hail, Macbeth and Banquo!

First Witch. Banquo and Macbeth, all hail!

70   **Macbeth.** Stay, you imperfect speakers. Tell me more.

---

[20]**happy:** fortunate (related to *happenstance* and *perhaps*).

[21]**get:** beget; be the ancestor of.

By Sinel's[22] death I know I am Thane of Glamis.

But how of Cawdor? The Thane of Cawdor lives

A prosperous gentleman, and to be king

Stands not within the prospect of belief,

75 No more than to be Cawdor. Say from whence

You owe this strange intelligence or why

Upon this blasted heath you stop our way

With such prophetic greeting. Speak, I charge you.

[Witches *vanish*.]

Banquo. The earth hath bubbles, as the water has,

80 And these are of them. Whither are they vanished?

Macbeth. Into the air, and what seemed **corporal** melted,

As breath into the wind. Would they had stayed!

Banquo. Were such things here as we do speak about?

Or have we eaten on the insane root

85 That takes the reason prisoner?

Macbeth. Your children shall be kings.

Banquo.   You shall be king.

Macbeth. And Thane of Cawdor too. Went it not so?

Banquo. To th' selfsame tune and words.—Who's here?

corporal:

---

[22]**Sinel:** Macbeth's father.

---

8. **◀ REREAD** Reread lines 39–47 and 70–78. How do Banquo's reactions to the witches differ from Macbeth's? What does Macbeth's reaction suggest about his character? Support your response with explicit textual evidence.

_____

_____

_____

_____

9. **READ ▶** As you read lines 89–127, continue to cite textual evidence.

- Circle what Macbeth and Banquo learn that confirms the witches' statements.
- Underline the moment Macbeth's feelings seem to change and intensify.
- In the margin, describe Macbeth's new feelings.

[*Enter* Ross *and* Angus.]

Ross. The King hath happily received, Macbeth,

90   The news of thy success, and, when he reads

Thy personal venture in the rebels' fight,

His wonders and his praises do contend

Which should be thine or his. Silenced with that,

In viewing o'er the rest o' th' selfsame day

95   He finds thee in the stout Norweyan ranks,

Nothing afeard of what thyself didst make,

Strange images of death. As thick as hail

Came post with post, and every one did bear

Thy praises in his kingdom's great defense,

100   And poured them down before him.

Angus.   We are sent

To give thee from our royal master thanks,

Only to herald thee into his sight,

Not pay thee.

Ross. And for an earnest[23] of a greater honor,

105   He bade me, from him, call thee Thane of Cawdor,

In which addition, hail, most worthy thane,

For it is thine.

Banquo.   What, can the devil speak true?

Macbeth. The Thane of Cawdor lives. Why do you dress me

In borrowed robes?

Angus.   Who was the Thane lives yet,

110   But under heavy judgment bears that life

Which he deserves to lose. Whether he was combined[24]

With those of Norway, or did line[25] the rebel

With hidden help and vantage, or that with both

He labored in his country's wrack, I know not;

115   But treasons capital, confessed and proved,

Have overthrown him.

Macbeth. [*Aside*]   Glamis and Thane of Cawdor!

The greatest is behind.[26] [*To Ross and* Angus] Thanks for your pains.

[*Aside to* Banquo] Do you not hope your children shall be kings

When those that gave the Thane of Cawdor to me

120   Promised no less to them?

---

[23]**earnest:** partial payment.
[24]**combined:** allied.
[25]**line:** support.
[26]**behind:** yet to come.

Banquo.   That, trusted home,[27]

Might yet enkindle you[28] unto the crown,

Besides the Thane of Cawdor. But 'tis strange.

And oftentimes, to win us to our harm,

The instruments of darkness tell us truths,

125   Win us with honest trifles, to betray 's

In deepest consequence.—

Cousins, a word, I pray you.   [*They step aside.*]

Macbeth. [*Aside*]   Two truths are told

As happy prologues to the swelling act

Of the imperial theme.—I thank you, gentlemen.

130   [*Aside*] This supernatural soliciting

Cannot be ill, cannot be good. If ill,

Why hath it given me earnest of success

Commencing in a truth? I am Thane of Cawdor.

If good, why do I yield to that suggestion

135   Whose horrid image doth unfix my hair

And make my seated heart knock at my ribs

---

[27]**home:** fully.

[28]**enkindle you:** inflame your ambitions.

---

10.   **◄ REREAD**   Reread Scene 3, lines 116–127. Contrast Macbeth's and
      Banquo's reactions to the realization that the first of the witches
      prophecies has come true. Support your answer with explicit textual
      evidence.

_____

_____

_____

_____

_____

11.   **READ ▶**   As you read Scene 3, lines 128–156, continue to cite textual
      evidence.

      • Circle the text that shows Macbeth's conflicting feelings about the
        witches' prophecy. In the margin, explain what Macbeth is thinking.

      • In the margin, tell what Macbeth's comment about chance shows about
        the kind of action he thinks about taking at this moment (lines 143–144).

Against the use of nature? Present fears
Are less than horrible imaginings.
My thought, whose murder yet is but fantastical,
140   Shakes so my single state of man
That function is smothered in surmise,
And nothing is but what is not.

Banquo.   Look how our partner's rapt.

Macbeth. [*Aside*] If chance will have me king, why, chance may crown me
Without my stir.[29]

Banquo.   New honors come upon him,
145   Like our strange garments, cleave not to their mold
But with the aid of use.

Macbeth. [*Aside*]   Come what come may,
Time and the hour runs through the roughest day.

Banquo. Worthy Macbeth, we stay upon your leisure.

Macbeth. Give me your favor. My dull brain was wrought
150   With things forgotten. Kind gentlemen, your pains
Are registered where every day I turn
The leaf to read them. Let us toward the King.
[*Aside to* Banquo] Think upon what hath chanced, and at more time,
The interim having weighed it, let us speak
155   Our free hearts each to other.

Banquo.   Very gladly.

Macbeth. Till then, enough.—Come, friends.
[*They exit.*]

---

[29] **my stir:** my doing anything.

12.   **◀ REREAD AND DISCUSS**   Reread Scene 3, lines 128–156. In a small group, discuss the influences of fate and ambition on Macbeth. Cite evidence from the text in your discussion.

13.   **READ ▷**   As you read Scene 4, lines 1–58, cite textual evidence.

- In the margin, explain why Malcolm's speech reminds the audience of the theme of betrayal (lines 2–11).
- Underline the passage that throws doubt on Duncan's judge of character.
- Underline Duncan's announcement in lines 35–39 and circle Macbeth's reaction in lines 48–53.

Scene 4 • *A room in the king's palace at Forres.*

[*Flourish. Enter* King Duncan, Lennox, Malcolm, Donalbain, *and* Attendants.]

Duncan. Is execution done on Cawdor? Are not
Those in commission yet returned?

Malcolm.   My liege,
They are not yet come back. But I have spoke
With one that saw him die, who did report

5   That very frankly he confessed his treasons,
Implored your Highness' pardon, and set forth
A deep repentance. Nothing in his life
Became him like the leaving it. He died
As one that had been studied in his death

10 To throw away the dearest thing he owed[30]
As 'twere a careless trifle.

Duncan.   There's no art
To find the mind's construction in the face.
He was a gentleman on whom I built
An absolute trust.
[*Enter* Macbeth, Banquo, Ross, *and* Angus.]
                           O worthiest cousin,

15 The sin of my ingratitude even now
Was heavy on me. Thou art so far before
That swiftest wing of recompense is slow
To overtake thee. Would thou hadst less deserved,
That the proportion both of thanks and payment

20 Might have been mine! Only I have left to say,
More is thy due than more than all can pay.

Macbeth. The service and the loyalty I owe
In doing it pays itself. Your Highness' part
Is to receive our duties, and our duties

25 Are to your throne and state children and servants,
Which do but what they should by doing everything
Safe toward your love and honor.

---

[30]**owed:** owned.

Duncan.   Welcome hither.

I have begun to plant thee and will labor

To make thee full of growing.—Noble Banquo,

30 That hast no less deserved nor must be known

No less to have done so, let me enfold thee

And hold thee to my heart.

Banquo.   There, if I grow,

The harvest is your own.

Duncan.   My plenteous joys,

wanton: **Wanton** in fullness, seek to hide themselves

35 In drops of sorrow.—Sons, kinsmen, thanes,

And you whose places are the nearest, know

We will establish our estate[31] upon

Our eldest, Malcolm, whom we name hereafter

The Prince of Cumberland;[32] which honor must

40 Not unaccompanied invest him only,

But signs of nobleness, like stars, shall shine

On all deservers.—From hence to Inverness,[33]

And bind us further to you.

Macbeth. The rest is labor which is not used for you.

harbinger: 45 I'll be myself the **harbinger** and make joyful

The hearing of my wife with your approach.

So humbly take my leave.

Duncan.   My worthy Cawdor.

Macbeth. [*Aside*] The Prince of Cumberland! That is a step

On which I must fall down or else o'erleap,

50 For in my way it lies. Stars, hide your fires;

Let not light see my black and deep desires.

The eye wink at the hand, yet let that be

Which the eye fears, when it is done, to see.

[*He exits.*]

Duncan. True, worthy Banquo. He is full so valiant,

55 And in his commendations I am fed:

It is a banquet to me.—Let's after him,

Whose care is gone before to bid us welcome.

It is a peerless kinsman.

[*Flourish. They exit.*]

---

[31]**estate:** succession of heirs.

[32]**The Prince of Cumberland:** the title given to the heir of the Scottish throne.

[33]**Inverness:** Macbeth's castle; it was an honor to have the king visit one's home.

Scene 5 • *Macbeth's castle at Inverness.*

[*Enter* Lady Macbeth, *alone, with a letter.*]

Lady Macbeth. [*Reading the letter*] "They met me in the day of success, and I have learned by the perfect'st report they have more in them than mortal knowledge. When I burned in desire to question them further, they made themselves air, into which they vanished. Whiles I stood rapt
5 in the wonder of it came missives from the King, who all-hailed me 'Thane of Cawdor,' by which title, before, these Weïrd Sisters saluted me and referred me to the coming on of time with 'Hail, king that shalt be.' This have I thought good to deliver thee, my dearest partner of greatness, that thou might'st not lose the dues of rejoicing by being
10 ignorant of what greatness is promised thee. Lay it to thy heart, and farewell."

   Glamis thou art, and Cawdor, and shalt be
What thou art promised. Yet do I fear thy nature;
It is too full o' th' milk of human kindness
15 To catch the nearest way. Thou wouldst be great,
Art not without ambition, but without
The illness[34] should attend it. What thou wouldst highly,
That wouldst thou holily;[35] wouldst not play false
And yet wouldst wrongly win. Thou'd'st have, great Glamis,

---

[34]**illness:** wickedness, ruthlessness.
[35]**holily:** virtuously.

---

14. **◀ REREAD** Reread Scene 4, lines 48–53. What does Macbeth admit in this aside? Based on these lines, what do you think is Macbeth's tragic flaw? Cite text evidence in your response.

_____

_____

_____

_____

15. **READ ▶** As you read Scene 5, lines 1–51, continue to cite textual evidence.

   • In the margin, sum up Lady Macbeth's misgivings about her husband (lines 13–15).

   • In the margin, list some adjectives that describe Lady Macbeth's character (lines 35–51). Explain what she is asking for in this soliloquy.

20   That which cries "Thus thou must do," if thou have it,

And that which rather thou dost fear to do,

Than wishest should be undone. Hie thee hither,

That I may pour my spirits in thine ear

And chastise with the valor of my tongue

25   All that impedes thee from the golden round

Which fate and metaphysical aid doth seem

To have thee crowned withal.

[*Enter* Messenger.]

What is your tidings?

Messenger. The King comes here tonight.

Lady Macbeth.   Thou'rt mad to say it!

Is not thy master with him? who, were't so,

30   Would have informed for preparation.

Messenger. So please you, it is true. Our Thane is coming.

One of my fellows had the speed of him,

Who, almost dead for breath, had scarcely more

Than would make up his message.

Lady Macbeth.   Give him tending.

35   He brings great news.

[Messenger *exits.*]

The raven[36] himself is hoarse

That croaks the fatal entrance of Duncan

Under my battlements. Come, you spirits

That tend on mortal thoughts, unsex me here,

And fill me from the crown to the toe top-full

40   Of direst cruelty. Make thick my blood.

Stop up th' access and passage to remorse,

That no compunctious visitings of nature[37]

Shake my fell purpose, nor keep peace between

Th' effect and it. Come to my woman's breasts

45   And take my milk for gall,[38] you murd'ring ministers,[39]

Wherever in your sightless[40] substances

You wait on nature's mischief. Come, thick night,

And pall[41] thee in the dunnest smoke of hell,

---

[36] **raven:** a bird that often symbolizes evil or misfortune.
[37] **compunctious visitings of nature:** the natural pangs of a guilty conscience.
[38] **gall:** bile, a bitter substance produced by the liver.
[39] **ministers:** agents.
[40] **sightless:** invisible.
[41] **pall:** wrap, cover.

That my keen knife see not the wound it makes,

50   Nor heaven peep through the blanket of the dark

To cry "Hold, hold!"

[*Enter* Macbeth.]

Great Glamis, worthy Cawdor,

Greater than both by the all-hail hereafter!

Thy letters have transported me beyond

This ignorant present, and I feel now

55   The future in the instant.

Macbeth.   My dearest love,

Duncan comes here tonight.

Lady Macbeth.   And when goes hence?

Macbeth. Tomorrow, as he purposes.

Lady Macbeth.   O, never

Shall sun that morrow see!

Your face, my thane, is as a book where men

60   May read strange matters. To beguile the time,

Look like the time. Bear welcome in your eye,

Your hand, your tongue. Look like th' innocent flower,

But be the serpent under 't. He that's coming

Must be provided for; and you shall put

65   This night's great business into my dispatch,[42]

Which shall to all our nights and days to come

Give solely sovereign sway and masterdom.

Macbeth. We will speak further.

Lady Macbeth.   Only look up clear.

To alter favor ever is to fear.[43]

70   Leave all the rest to me.

[*They exit.*]

---

[42]**dispatch:** management.

[43]**to alter favor ever is to fear:** to change expression (**favor**) is a sign of fear.

---

16. ◄ **REREAD AND DISCUSS** Reread Scene 5, lines 12–27, and 35–51. With a small group, discuss the kind of woman revealed in these speeches. How does she feel about her husband? What motivates her plans for the future?

17. **READ** ▷ As you read Scene 5, lines 52–70, continue to cite textual evidence.

   • Underline the words that Lady Macbeth uses to greet her husband. Then, circle the way Macbeth addresses Lady Macbeth when he first sees her.

   • In the margin, explain what their greetings say about their relationship.

Scene 6 • *In front of Macbeth's castle.*

[*Hautboys and Torches. Enter* King Duncan, Malcolm, Donalbain, Banquo, Lennox, Macduff, Ross, Angus, *and* Attendants.]

Duncan. This castle hath a pleasant seat. The air
Nimbly and sweetly recommends itself
Unto our gentle senses.

Banquo.   This guest of summer,
The temple-haunting martlet,[44] does approve,
5   By his loved mansionry, that the heaven's breath
Smells wooingly here. No jutty, frieze,
Buttress, nor coign of vantage, but this bird
Hath made his pendant bed and procreant cradle.
Where they most breed and haunt, I have observed,
10   The air is delicate.

[*Enter* Lady Macbeth.]

Duncan.   See, see, our honored hostess!—
The love that follows us sometime is our trouble,
Which still we thank as love. Herein I teach you
How you shall bid God 'ield[45] us for your pains

---

[44]**martlet:** a house martin—a small bird that often nests on buildings such as churches.
[45]**'ield:** yield (i.e., thank you).

---

18. **◄ REREAD** Reread Scene 5, lines 56–70. Compare the intensity of ambition displayed by Macbeth and Lady Macbeth. Which one seems more likely to commit to a murderous plan? Support your response with explicit text evidence.

_____

_____

_____

_____

19. **READ ▶** As you read Scene 6, lines 1–31, continue to cite textual evidence.

• Underline the positive, benevolent images of nature that Duncan and Banquo use.

• In the margin, explain why this imagery is an example of dramatic irony (lines 1–10).

> ## The love that follows us sometime is our trouble, Which still we thank as love.

And thank us for your trouble.

Lady Macbeth.   All our service,

15 In every point twice done and then done double,
Were poor and single business to contend
Against those honors deep and broad wherewith
Your Majesty loads our house. For those of old,
And the late dignities heaped up to them,

20 We rest your hermits.[46]

Duncan.   Where's the Thane of Cawdor?
We coursed him at the heels and had a purpose
To be his purveyor; but he rides well,
And his great love (sharp as his spur) hath helped him
To his home before us. Fair and noble hostess,

25 We are your guest tonight.

Lady Macbeth.   Your servants ever
Have theirs, themselves, and what is theirs in compt
To make their audit at your Highness' pleasure,
Still to return your own.

Duncan.   Give me your hand.

[*Taking her hand*]

Conduct me to mine host. We love him highly

30 And shall continue our graces towards him.
By your leave, hostess.

[*They exit.*]

---

[46]**hermits:** we (**as hermits**) will pray for you. Hermits were often paid to pray for another's soul.

---

20. ◀ REREAD Reread Scene 6, lines 10–31. Compare and contrast the words of King Duncan and those of Lady Macbeth. Support your answer with explicit textual evidence.

_____

_____

_____

Scene 7 • *A room in Macbeth's castle.*

[*Hautboys. Torches. Enter a Sewer, and divers* Servants[47] *with dishes and service over the stage. Then enter* Macbeth.]

Macbeth. If it were done when 'tis done, then 'twere well
It were done quickly. If th' assassination
Could trammel up the consequence and catch
With his surcease[48] success, that but this blow

5   Might be the be-all and the end-all here,
But here, upon this bank and shoal of time,
We'd jump the life to come. But in these cases
We still have judgment here, that we but teach
Bloody instructions, which, being taught, return

10 To plague th' inventor. This even-handed justice
Commends th' ingredience of our poisoned chalice
To our own lips. He's here in double trust:
First, as I am his kinsman and his subject,
Strong both against the deed; then, as his host,

15 Who should against his murderer shut the door,
Not bear the knife myself. Besides, this Duncan
Hath borne his faculties so meek, hath been
So clear in his great office, that his virtues
Will plead like angels, trumpet-tongued, against

20 The deep damnation of his taking-off;
And pity, like a naked newborn babe
Striding the blast, or heaven's cherubin horsed
Upon the sightless couriers of the air,
Shall blow the horrid deed in every eye,

---

[47]**Hautboys . . . a Sewar, and divers Servants:** oboes (**hautboys**) . . . a steward, or servant responsible for arranging the banquet (**sewer**), and various (**divers**) servants.
[48]**surcease:** completion.

---

21. **READ ▶** As you read Scene 7, lines 1–45, continue to cite textual evidence.

• Underline Macbeth's reasons for not harming Duncan.
• In the margin, sum up the conversation between Macbeth and Lady Macbeth (lines 31–45).

> "If it were done
> when 'tis done,
> then 'twere well
> It were done quickly."

25   That tears shall drown the wind. I have no spur
      To prick the sides of my intent, but only
      Vaulting ambition, which o'erleaps itself
      And falls on th' other—
      [*Enter* Lady Macbeth.]
                                    How now? What news?
      Lady Macbeth. He has almost supped.
      Why have you left the chamber?
30   **Macbeth.** Hath he asked for me?
      Lady Macbeth.   Know you not he has?
      Macbeth. We will proceed no further in this business.
      He hath honored me of late, and I have bought
      Golden opinions from all sorts of people,
      Which would be worn now in their newest gloss,
35   Not cast aside so soon.
      Lady Macbeth.   Was the hope[49] drunk
      Wherein you dressed yourself? Hath it slept since?
      And wakes it now, to look so green and pale
      At what it did so freely? From this time
      Such I account thy love. Art thou afeard
40   To be the same in thine own act and valor
      As thou art in desire? Wouldst thou have that
      Which thou esteem'st the ornament of life

      _____
      [49] **hope:** ambition.

22. ◀ REREAD Reread Scene 7, lines 12–28 and lines 31–35. What does
    Macbeth's reasoning show about his state of mind? Cite explicit text evidence
    in your response.

    _____

    _____

    _____

And live a coward in thine own esteem,

Letting "I dare not" wait upon "I would,"

45   Like the poor cat i' th' adage?[50]

Macbeth.   Prithee, peace.

I dare do all that may become a man.

Who dares do more is none.

Lady Macbeth.   What beast was't, then,

That made you break this enterprise to me?

When you durst[51] do it, then you were a man;

50   And to be more than what you were, you would

Be so much more the man. Nor time nor place

Did then adhere,[52] and yet you would make both.

They have made themselves, and that their fitness now

Does unmake you. I have given suck, and know

55   How tender 'tis to love the babe that milks me.

I would, while it was smiling in my face,

Have plucked my nipple from his boneless gums

And dashed the brains out, had I so sworn as you

Have done to this.

Macbeth.   If we should fail—

Lady Macbeth.   We fail?

60   But screw your courage to the sticking place

And we'll not fail. When Duncan is asleep

(Whereto the rather shall his day's hard journey

Soundly invite him), his two chamberlains

Will I with wine and wassail so convince

65   That memory, the warder of the brain,

---

[50]**poor cat i' th' adage:** a cat in a proverb (**adage**) that wouldn't catch fish because it feared wet feet.

[51]**durst:** dared.

[52]**adhere:** agree.

23. **READ** ▶ As you read lines 46–82, continue to cite text evidence.

- In the margin, summarize what Lady Macbeth says to urge Macbeth to act (lines 47–59).
- In the margin, explain how Lady Macbeth plans to accomplish the deed and avoid suspicion (lines 59–72).
- In the margin, make an inference about the way Macbeth feels about his wife (lines 72–77).

Shall be a fume, and the receipt of reason
A limbeck[53] only. When in swinish sleep
Their drenchèd natures lie as in a death,
What cannot you and I perform upon
70   Th' unguarded Duncan? What not put upon
His spongy officers, who shall bear the guilt
Of our great quell?
    Macbeth.   Bring forth men-children only,
For thy undaunted mettle[54] should compose
Nothing but males. Will it not be received,
75   When we have marked with blood those sleepy two
Of his own chamber and used their very daggers,
That they have done 't?
    Lady Macbeth.   Who dares receive it other,
As we shall make our griefs and clamor roar
Upon his death?
    Macbeth.   I am settled and bend up
80   Each corporal agent to this terrible feat.
Away, and mock the time with fairest show.
False face must hide what the false heart doth know.
[*They exit.*]

---

[53]**limbeck:** a still for making liquor.
[54]**mettle:** spirit.

24. **◄ REREAD**   Reread lines 46–82. How would you characterize Lady Macbeth's way of arguing? How effective is she in getting what she wants? Cite explicit text evidence in your response.

_____

_____

_____

_____

_____

SHORT RESPONSE

Cite Text Evidence   What forces and influences, external and internal, drive Macbeth toward his final decision at the end of Scene 7? In what ways does he try to withstand the urge to act against Duncan? **Cite text evidence** in your response.

_____

_____

_____

_____

_____

_____

_____

_____

_____

_____

_____

_____

Hard-Won Liberty

COLLECTION **6**
Hard-Won Liberty

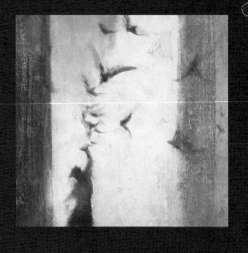

"There is no easy walk to freedom anywhere."

—Nelson Mandela

SPEECH
Speech at the March on Washington

Josephine Baker

SHORT STORY
Bile

Christine Lee Zilka

Background Josephine Baker *(1906–1975) was an African American dancer and singer who became an international musical and political icon. After dropping out of high school, Baker joined a vaudeville troupe as a dancer and headed to New York City. In the 1920s, she moved to France, where she became an overnight sensation, dancing and singing in cabarets. In the 1950s and 1960s, she joined the fight for civil rights, refusing to perform for segregated audiences and eventually adopting 12 multiethnic children. In 1963, Baker was asked to speak at the March on Washington, along with Martin Luther King, Jr. and other civil rights leaders.*

Speech at the March on Washington

Speech by Josephine Baker

© Houghton Mifflin Harcourt Publishing Company • Image Credits: ©Bettmann/Corbis

CLOSE READ
Notes

1. **READ ▷** As you read lines 1–13, begin to collect and cite text evidence.

   - Underline the statement Baker gives to introduce herself.
   - In the margin, explain Baker's reasons for speaking out.
   - Circle the difference between Josephine Baker and other African Americans.

Friends and family . . . you know I have lived a long time and I have come a long way. And you must know now that what I did, I did originally for myself. Then later, as these things began happening to me, I wondered if they were happening to you, and then I knew they must be. And I knew that you had no way to defend yourselves, as I had.

And as I continued to do the things I did, and to say the things I said, they began to beat me. Not beat me, mind you, with a club—but you know, I have seen that done too—but they beat me with their pens, with their writings. And friends, that is much worse.

10   When I was a child and they burned me out of my home, I was frightened and I ran away. Eventually I ran far away. It was to a place called France. Many of you have been there, and many have not. But I must tell you, ladies and gentlemen, in that country I never feared.

But I must tell you, when I was young in Paris, strange things happened to me. And these things had never happened to me before. When I left St. Louis a long time ago, the conductor directed me to the last car. And you all know what that means.

But when I ran away, yes, when I ran away to another country, I didn't have to do that. I could go into any restaurant I wanted to, and I could drink water anyplace I wanted to, and I didn't have to go to a colored toilet either, and I have to tell you it was nice, and I got used to it, and I liked it, and I wasn't afraid anymore that someone would shout at me and say, "Go to the end of the line."

So over there, far away, I was happy, and because I was happy I had some success, and you know that too.

Then, after a long time, I came to America to be in a great show for Mr. Ziegfeld,[1] and you know Josephine was happy. You know that. Because I wanted to tell everyone in my country about myself. I wanted to let everyone know that I made good, and you know too that that is only natural.

But on that great big beautiful ship, I had a bad experience. A very important star was to sit with me for dinner, and at the last moment I discovered she didn't want to eat with a colored woman. I can tell you it was some blow.

And I won't bother to mention her name, because it is not important, and anyway, now she is dead.

---

[1] **Mr. Ziegfeld:** Florenz Ziegfeld (1867–1932) was an American theater producer known for his series of theatrical revues called the Ziegfeld Follies.

2. **REREAD** Reread lines 6–13. What are the most important points Baker makes in these lines?

_____

_____

_____

_____

3. **READ** As you read lines 14–41, continue to cite textual evidence.

• Underline examples of segregation in America.

• In the margin, explain why Baker was happier in France (lines 18–30).

And when I got to New York way back then, I had other blows—when they would not let me check into the good hotels because I was colored, or eat in certain restaurants. And then I went to Atlanta, and it was a horror to

40 me. And I said to myself, I am Josephine, and if they do this to me, what do they do to the other people in America?

You know, friends, that I do not lie to you when I tell you I have walked into the palaces of kings and queens and into the houses of presidents. And much more. But I could not walk into a hotel in America and get a cup of coffee, and that made me mad. And when I get mad, you know that I open my big mouth. And then look out, 'cause when Josephine opens her mouth, they hear it all over the world.

So I did open my mouth, and you know I did scream, and when I demanded what I was supposed to have and what I was entitled to, they still

50 would not give it to me.

So then they thought they could smear me, and the best way to do that was to call me a communist. And you know, too, what that meant. Those were dreaded words in those days, and I want to tell you also that I was hounded by the government agencies in America, and there was never one ounce of proof that I was a communist. But they were mad. They were mad because I told the truth. And the truth was that all I wanted was a cup of coffee. But I wanted that cup of coffee where *I* wanted to drink it, and I had the money to pay for it, so why shouldn't I have it where I wanted it?

4. **◀ REREAD** Reread lines 37–41. Explain Josephine Baker's thinking in these lines. Why is she concerned with "the other people in America"?

_____

_____

_____

_____

_____

_____

5. **READ ▶** As you read lines 42–58, continue to cite textual evidence.

• In the margin, explain why Josephine Baker "opens her mouth."

• Underline text that explains what happened as a result of Baker's protests.

Friends and brothers and sisters, that is how it went. And when I
60 screamed loud enough, they started to open that door just a little bit, and
we all started to be able to squeeze through it.

Now, I am not going to stand in front of all of you today and take credit
for what is happening now. I cannot do that. But I want to take credit for
telling you how to do the same thing, and when you scream, friends, I know
you will be heard. And you will be heard now.

But you young people must do one thing, and I know you have heard
this story a thousand times from your mothers and fathers, like I did from
my mama. I didn't take her advice. But I accomplished the same in another
fashion. You must get an education. You must go to school, and you must
70 learn to protect yourself. And you must learn to protect yourself with the
pen, and not the gun. Then you can answer them, and I can tell you—and I
don't want to sound corny—but friends, the pen really is mightier than the
sword.

• • •

6. **◄ REREAD** Reread lines 42–58. How does Baker's claim of the rights
afforded to her in other countries strengthen her argument? Support
your answer with explicit textual evidence.

_____

_____

_____

_____

_____

_____

_____

_____

7. **READ ►** As you read lines 59–78, continue to cite textual evidence.

• Underline text describing the results of Baker's "screaming."
• In the margin, explain Baker's advice for young people.
• Circle text describing the benefits of protecting oneself with a pen.

> " I want you to have a chance at what I had. But I do not want you to have to run away to get it. "

I am not a young woman now, friends. My life is behind me. There is not too much fire burning inside me. And before it goes out, I want you to use what is left to light that fire in you. So that you can carry on, and so that you can do those things that I have done. Then, when my fires have burned out, and I go where we all go someday, I can be happy.

80   You know, I have always taken the rocky path. I never took the easy one, but as I grew older, and as I knew I had the power and the strength, I took that rocky path, and I tried to smooth it out a little. I wanted to make it easier for you. I want you to have a chance at what I had. But I do not want you to have to run away to get it. And mothers and fathers, if it is too late for you, think of your children. Make it safe here so they do not have to run away, for I want for you and your children what I had.

8. **◀ REREAD** Reread lines 59–73. What does Josephine Baker give herself credit for in the civil rights movement? How does this reasoning appeal to the shared beliefs of her audience? Support your answer with explicit textual evidence.

_____

_____

_____

_____

_____

9. **READ ▶** As you read lines 79–96, continue to cite textual evidence.

• Underline text describing what Baker has done for African Americans.
• Circle text explaining what Josephine Baker asks the audience to do for future generations.

Ladies and gentlemen, my friends and family, I have just been handed a little note, as you probably saw. It is an invitation to visit the President of the United States in his home, the White House.

I am greatly honored. But I must tell you that a colored woman—or, as

90   you say it here in America, a black woman—is not going there. It is a woman. It is Josephine Baker.

It is a great honor for me. Someday I want you children out there to have that great honor too. And we know that that time is not someday. We know that that time is *now*.

I thank you, and may God bless you. And may He continue to bless you long after I am gone.

---

10. ◀ **REREAD AND DISCUSS** Reread lines 86–91. In a small group, discuss what Baker means by saying "a black woman—is not going there."

SHORT RESPONSE

Cite Text Evidence What universal themes does Baker explore in her speech? What makes these themes universal? Review your reading notes, and be sure to **cite text evidence** in your response.

_____

_____

_____

_____

_____

_____

_____

_____

_____

Background *In June 1950, Communist North Korea invaded South Korea and U.S. President Truman authorized the use of American ground forces to stop the advance. He felt it was necessary to intervene in order to take a stand against Communist aggression. After some early back-and-forth, the fighting stalled and casualties mounted. American officials worked anxiously with North Koreans to end the war. An agreement was finally reached in July 1953. In all, some 2.5 million soldiers and civilians lost their lives during the war.* **Christine Lee Zilka** *explores the repercussions the Korean War has on one American family in the following short story.*

Bile

Short Story by Christine Lee Zilka

1. **READ ▷** As you read lines 1–33, begin to collect and cite text evidence.

   - Underline text that references the war.
   - Circle text describing the family's background.
   - In the margin, explain what the narrator learns about her father in lines 19–22.

When the Korean War ended in 1953, my father became restless. Korea lay in ruins, but there were no more enemy soldiers and no more bombs to flee. My father had become addicted to war. Without battles, he had no sense of urgency, no sense of drama. He had already survived, and like the rest of the country, he tried to pick up his life where he had left off. But he was not used to peace. He could make no sense of math equations as an engineering student; it all seemed **trivial**.

trivial:

He made journeys into the countryside where he had grown up, hoping to reconnect himself. On one of his outings, he found a trapper gutting a
10 bear. An idea came to him. He asked the hunter for the gall bladder of the bear.

My father put his tongue to the gall bladder. It tasted like the war. He smiled grimly. He could not fail. He could not turn back, because behind him were the Japanese army, the North Korean army, poverty, and abuse.

bile:

He could not rest. This **bile** would be his medicine. He wrapped up the gall bladder and froze it. Whenever he felt he was getting too content, sleeping an hour too much, smiling a second too long, he would hunger for the taste of it, bitter, and clinging to his tongue.

20   As children, we learned that Daddy would have died if he had not had the bile: the bile reminded him of the misery and bitterness of suffering.

What I now realize is that the bitterness stayed inside him and traveled from his tongue, down into his belly, where it now churns.

Tradition runs strong in our family. We are Korean Americans, a strong line of warriors, descended from the Mongols. We are modern Genghis Khans,[1] quick tempered but passionate, with chronicles of suffering living in our veins. We are nomadic, settling in a country that severed our mother country in half, with a tourniquet of barbed wire, swathed in khaki green.

Suffering is so much a part of the Korean psyche that we have given it a word, *Han*. It is a particular suffering, a sense of helplessness against

30   overwhelming odds, a feeling of total abandonment. This word is part of what we call ourselves and our mother country, *Hankook sahrahm, Hankook nahrah*; Korean people, Korean land. This Han is silent and noble. It is our code and **mantra**.

mantra:

---

[1] **Genghis Khan:** (1162?–1227) Mongol conqueror who united the Mongol tribes and forged an empire from China to Persia.

---

2. ◀ REREAD   Reread lines 1–33. In your own words, summarize what you have learned about the narrator's father. Support your answer with explicit textual evidence.

_____

_____

_____

_____

_____

3. READ ▶   As you read lines 34–85, continue to cite text evidence.

- Underline text that characterizes Eugene or describes his actions.
- In the margin, explain what happens in lines 34–42.
- Circle text that characterizes the other three family members.

> ❝ I had hard life, nothing
> to look forward to, just
> running away. ❞

On our Sunday hikes, my father brings up the rear. My brother Eugene, the Boy Scout, bounds up the hill on light bunny feet. Safe on the hiking trails of the San Gabriel Mountains, I try to enjoy the views beyond the silt of smog, but Father barks at us, that there is an army behind us. We quicken our pace. There are sharp-toothed men who want to kill us. They have shotguns, horsehair hats. They ride bareback, puff on long pipes, smoke opium, stab each other in the back.

Eugene runs up the hill out of earshot. Father, Mother, and I drip with effort, and we push ourselves to each crest out of this ancestral fear.

"Eugene! Wait for us!" I shout. I don't see him anymore, and he doesn't answer. The path bends mercilessly in the chaparral[2] heat.

"Forget about him. He never wait. Stupid boy, never cares about us," says Father.

Mother hits Father on the arm. "Leave him alone. You are bossy, maybe he's running away from you."

Father glares. Mother doubles her pace so that her shoes kick dust back at us over the switchback.

Up ahead, I imagine Eugene's already arrived at the destination, a shady **plateau** of pine trees. He's taking a long sip of water from the water fountain up there, and drinking in the views of Pasadena. He may even see us, a short and irritated snake making its way.

We gather in the kitchen to eat an early lunch. Our bodies, sweaty with the recent Sunday excursion, stick to the vinyl kitchen seats. Father looks straight at Eugene, points his finger and bellows, "You never wait for us!"

Eugene rolls his eyes and says, "Dad, you never give us a break."

Father takes a breath and continues. "I am going to tell you about myself, your father. I had hard life, nothing to look forward to, just running away. Eugene, you run to something, like nothing pushing. We go hiking, you go away. You don't wait for your own family? We have to enjoy together!"

Eugene replied, "You were just slow, and I waited for you at the top. What's the big deal?" My brother kicks me in the leg.

I chime in. "Dad, please don't worry so much. It's not so complicated. Eugene just is in better shape. Don't take it so seriously. We get it!" (Please, please do not tell the story again.)

plateau:

---

[2] **chaparral:** a dense growth of tangled thorny shrubs.

"I gave up my dreams long ago and decided to have children instead.

70 You don't know your father, what I do for you! You know, I have to teach you good lesson, so you will never forget." This sends my father into a **synopsis** of his life. We have it memorized.

synopsis:

"I don't even know if my brother is alive. He fought against the Japanese, and they took everything, burned our house. I was five years old. But our family was a hero family, so our village supported us," says Father. "Then the Korean War came, and my brother, he joined the Communists. Everyone hated us then. We had to burn his pictures. Still, we survived."

So it was with my mother as well. "Your mommy, her family had to leave North Korea. They took only what they could carry. They put the

80 money and gold and jewelry inside their clothes, inside the silk linings. Rich people became poor in one night!"

Then Mother adds, "But we were smart. Instead of eating only one bowl of rice a day, we mixed it with barley, so we ate a little more often. We always ate, even though sometimes we had to sell our clothes. Your grandma's wedding dress, someone else owns it now."

"Eugene, you are going to learn," says Father. He nods at my mother, points at the refrigerator. My mother takes out a recycled plastic Safeway

---

4. **◀ REREAD**   Reread lines 34–85. Explain how Eugene acts differently from the rest of the family. Why is his father so upset? Support your answer with explicit textual evidence.

_____

_____

_____

_____

_____

_____

5. **READ ▶**   As you read lines 86–156, prepare to cite text evidence.

- Underline text that explains what the gall bladder and its bile represent to the parents.
- Circle text that shows the children's reactions to the gall bladder in lines 86–115.
- In the margin, explain what the father tells Eugene about the gall bladder in lines 94–100.

> "It does not send an alarm, but Eugene raises an eyebrow and I lean forward."

bag. We reuse plastic bags often, and it could contain anything, a box of ice cream or a package of dried seaweed. It does not send an alarm, but Eugene
90 raises an eyebrow and I lean forward.

"We have something for you. It will help you like it helped your father."

Eugene nods, distracted. "Enough with the story. I get it! I have heard it all before. You had a lousy childhood . . . "

"Don't say that! I don't think you understand. I took the gall bladder of a bear and drank the bile! It reminded me of what I was working away from. I was working so I would have a better future. So I would have a better future than my past. My past is bile! You have to learn about your father. Who you are, you know?"

"You have to be tough, too," comments Mother.
100 "You will learn, too," says Father.

Mother hands the plastic bag to me, and goes to get a plate from the cupboard. The bag hisses open. Inside is a Ziploc bag, and inside it is a piece of flesh. It looks slimy like the innards of Foster Farm chickens. But this is larger than any chicken liver I've ever seen. It is pear-shaped and bruised in tones of blue and gray and brown. It is dying, deflating, defecating on itself. I fully expect it to pulse, but it lies still. It smells like a goat has parked itself in our kitchen.

Father gestures to me. "Open it! Take it out! Put it on the plate!" I take out the Ziploc bag and place it gingerly on the plate. Is this some kind of
110 sick sushi?

"Open it!" snaps Mother.

I recoil. Mother and Father are on some screwed-up Old World kick, and I duck out of view.

"I won't make you drink it like I did. You're not like me. You will taste it, that's all you need to do. But you will learn."

I can only tell you the before and the after, because I did not watch them feed Eugene the bile.

I leave the room. I hear my mother unwrap the gall bladder and snag it with chopsticks. I hear Eugene's footsteps, my father's commands, the rush of water from the faucet. I imagine the bile as it fills Eugene's body with poison and drains his face of all the pink flesh, leaving it pinched and brittle.

taut:

In the hallway outside the kitchen, I am surrounded by childhood awards and family pictures: Father smokes thin white cigarettes, leaning against a white tree trunk with dark gray leaves. He is wearing black pants and a white undershirt. He is lean and tanned. His shoulders are held back at attention, and his skin is **taut**, his eyes open wide. His gaze rests on something soft and gentle. He is at the point of remembering . . .

There's a picture of me at Disneyland, holding an ice cream cone. My father has no pictures of himself as a child, and maybe that furthers the distance between us, because we have no proof that he was ever a child. He was born a jaw-clenching, wide-eyed man who drank bile.

Eugene brushes past me in the hall. "Move," he says.

I move. "Hey."

He looks up and past me.

"Never mind," I say. There are no words of healing.

In this way, we inherit suffering. But the bile does not strengthen Eugene. It flows within him, as it did within my father, but it does not give him strength and resolve. Only resentment.

Long after the gallbladder has become a solid rock of ice next to the ice cream, Father asks me, "Should you taste the bile, too?"

I want to shout, "No!" but I don't. I want to tell him that I think this is sick and perverted, but I don't. I know what I have to say. Like my father, I know how to survive.

I know the answer to this. My father coached me a million times.

"I'm a Hankook sahrahm. I understand why I need this bile, because I already have this bile."

Father nods. He walks out of the kitchen, his feet squeaking against the linoleum.

He leaves a wake of anger in his path, and my mother and I sponge it up. We don't want him to return and refuel; it's easier when he does not see what he does to us, even though I think he should. I sit on the stool and stare out the windows into the cul de sac.

Mother scurries around, washing dishes. "You know your father, he really lives just for you. He really loves you, but it comes out all wrong," she apologizes. I stare at her Han figure.

I walk into the backyard and stare at the wall, covered in honeysuckle. The scent is sweet, and the drunken bees lumber slowly through the vines. The sun beats against me, and my plastic sandals mold against my feet and
160   stick slightly to the concrete path as they make "smuck-smuck" sounds on the patio pavers.

I've walked into a fireplace and I just want a little relief. I wonder what would happen if I could disappear. I wonder how mad my father would be. The neighbors' wall looms just ahead.

I drag one of the backyard benches over to the wall, and I sit in its shade. I cannot stay sitting for long. I stand on the bench to look over the wall into the neighbors' backyard. The Andersons are away on vacation, and we are on neighborhood watch.

Inside the house, I hear my father yelling at Eugene. Doors slam. My
170   mother makes kitchen noises, the clattering of dishes on countertop tile and porcelain sink. All this, amidst the bees and heat. I can either go inside the cool, poisonous house or melt outside.

My legs twitch. I've been standing still, stretched over the wall, and I ache. I have also been holding my breath. I let out a desperate exhalation. The Andersons' lot is on a higher elevation than ours; it would not be a long

---

6. **◄ REREAD** Reread lines 116–156. Summarize the narrator's response to her father's anger and his behavior. Support your answer with explicit textual evidence.

_____

_____

_____

_____

_____

_____

_____

7. **READ ▶** As you read lines 157–184, continue to cite text evidence.

• In the margin, explain the narrator's conflict in lines 162–172.

• Underline text describing the narrator's desires.

• Circle text that describes a change in the narrator in lines 179–184.

fall from the wall. I climb the wall slowly, so as not to anger the venomous bees, but I'm stung before I swing my leg over the top and fall into the Andersons' yard.

I limp to one of the lounge chairs and sit down. There's a welt on my leg
180 with a stinger pulsating in the middle of it. I pull it out, but the pain is still there. A dark part of me wells up and receives that pain. Out of my numbness arises the **cathartic** pain of a bee sting. It loosens the knot in my belly. I can breathe a little now. If I focus on the pain enough, the knot travels a little up my throat.

cathartic:

8. **◄ REREAD** Reread lines 157–161. What do you think the honeysuckle and the bees represent? Support your answer with explicit textual evidence.

_____

_____

_____

_____

SHORT RESPONSE

Cite Text Evidence How do parallels between the characterizations of the narrator and the father point to a theme of the story? Review your reading notes, and **cite text evidence** in your response.

_____

_____

_____

_____

_____

_____

_____

Acknowledgments

"Bile" by Christine Lee Zilka from *Zyzzyva,* January 30, 2012, *www.zyzzyva.org.* Text copyright © 2003 by Christine Lee Zilka. Reprinted by permission of Christine Lee Zilka.

"Emma Marris: In Defense of Everglades Pythons" by Emma Marris from *The New York Times*, August 17, 2012. Text copyright © 2012 by The New York Times. Reprinted by permission of PARS International on behalf of The New York Times. All rights reserved.

"Every Second Counts" by Matilda Battersby from *The Independent,* May 29, 2012, *www.independent.co.uk.* Text copyright © 2012 by The Independent. Reprinted by permission of The Independent.

"Preamble from the Universal Declaration of Human Rights" (retitled from "Preamble to the Universal Declaration of Human Rights") by the United Nations, December 10, 1948. Text copyright © 1948 by United Nations. Reprinted by permission of United Nations Publication Board.

Excerpt from "Presidential Address to the ANC Transvaal Congress, 9/21/53," also known as the "No easy walk to freedom" speech, by Nelson Mandela, quoting Jawaharlal Nehru. Text copyright © 1953 by Nelson Mandela. Reprinted by permission of the Nelson Mandela Foundation.

"Sea Stars" (retitled from "Sea Stars: A Galaxy at Our Feet") by Barbara Hurd from *Orion*, May/June 2008, *www.orionmagazine.org.* Text copyright © 2008 by University of Georgia Press. Reprinted by permission of University of Georgia Press.

Excerpt from "The Seventh Man" from *Blind Willow, Sleeping Woman* by Haruki Murakami. Text copyright © 2006 by Haruki Murakami. Reprinted by permission of International Creative Management, Inc.

"Speech at the March on Washington" excerpted and titled from *Remembering Josephine* by Stephen Papich. Text copyright © by Bennetta Jules-Rossette. Reprinted by permission of Bennetta Jules-Rossette.

"Starfish" from *Emplumada* by Lorna Dee Cervantes. Text copyright © 1982 by Lorna Dee Cervantes. Reprinted by permission of University of Pittsburgh Press.

"The Starry Night" from *The Complete Poems* by Anne Sexton. Text copyright © 1981 Linda Gray Sexton and Loring Conant, Jr., executors of the will of Anne Sexton. Reprinted by permission of Houghton Mifflin Harcourt Publishing Company and Sterling Lord Literistic, Inc.

"Today" from *Nine Horses,* by Billy Collins. Text copyright © 2002 by Billy Collins. Reprinted by permission of Random House, Inc. Any third party use of this material, outside of this publication, is prohibited. Interested parties must apply directly to Random House, Inc. for permission.

Excerpt from "Towards a True Refuge" from *Freedom from Fear and Other Writings, Revised Edition* by Aung San Suu Kyi, foreword by Vaclav Havel, translated by Michael Aris. Text copyright © 1991, 1995 by Aung San Suu Kyi and Michael Aris. Reprinted by permission of Penguin Group UK and Viking Penguin, a division of Penguin Group (USA) Inc.

"The Trouble with Poetry" from *The Trouble with Poetry and Other Poems* by Billy Collins. Text copyright © 2005 by Billy Collins. Reprinted by permission of Random House, Inc. Any third party use of this material, outside of this publication, is prohibited. Interested parties must apply directly to Random House, Inc. for permission.

"Whale Sharks Use Geometry to Avoid Sinking" from *www.ScienceDaily.com,* Nov. 27, 2010. Reprinted by permission of John Wiley & Sons, Inc. and ScienceDaily. Source: "Moved by that sinking feeling: variable diving geometry underlies movement strategies in whale sharks" by Adrian C. Gleiss, Brad Norman, and Rory P. Wilson from Functional Ecology, 2010; DOI: 10.1111/j.1365–2435.2010.01801.x.

"The Wife's Story" from *The Compass Rose: Stories* by Ursula K. Le Guin. Text copyright © 1982 by Ursula K. Le Guin. Reprinted by permission of Ursula K. Le Guin and the author's agents, the Virginia Kidd Literary Agency, Inc.

Index of Titles & Authors